Villa Carlotta the Garden and the Museum

Historical-artistic Guide

Texts by
Paolo Cottini
Paola Zatti

Silvana Editoriale

*T*he building of the villa began three hundred years ago, in 1690, and since then it has intimately, however submissively, been linked to the social and economic life, to the wealth and decadence of the families that have owned it, three in number up to the end of World War I: the Clericis, the Sommarivas, and the Sassonia Meinengens.

Its magnificent, but ever-private, residence-like nature confers to the villa the charm of what is lived-in, humanizing the austerity of the museum, and the meticulously scientific order of the botanical garden, transforming the visitor into a guest. This, along with the mild and splendid nature of Lake Como, is the reason why each year more than one hundred thousand vistors, both Italian and foreign, come to visit the villa.

Architecture and art are manifested in the villa in a thousand ways and through the use of the most diverse materials—from stone to the plants of the flower-beds—uniting to the point that they nearly become indistinguishable. It is not by chance that the villa has no 'architect,' but seems to have been born and raised nourished by the love of its owners, who certainly felt that it was 'theirs,' and wanted it to be more and more beautiful and harmonious.

At the end of World War I it was Giuseppe Bianchini, a lawyer, the count of Lenno and senator of the Kingdom, with the help of his fellow members of the Rotary Club of Milan, who wrote the Society's constitution, which is still today entrusted with the preservation of the villa. By so doing he saved it from being auctioned off, that would undoubtedly have led to its dismantling. The twenties were rushing by, and if we read the accounts of those times—filled with social upheaval, political crisis, economic concerns—it is hard to believe that at such a dramatic time in the history of our country anyone could find the time and the will to safeguard an environmental and artistic wealth that was marginal if compared to the national scene.

And yet once again, culture—meaning the highest expression of civilization and love for what is 'beautiful'—overcame daily concerns and found resources and support to bring about its plan. The same love—together with the respect for an equilibrium that only the slow metabolism of changes over time have known how to guarantee—animates that which today is called to preserve for the future generations this wealth, the expression of a profoundly European civilization.

It is not an easy task. It is necessary to square the accounts without giving in to temptations of a managerial sort, that would want the villa to be transformed into a location for performances and meetings which are certainly remunerative, but that can at the same time be devastating; we must without visible trauma renew an arboreal wealth that gets older every year, but that takes decades to be accomplished; we must restore and preserve with delicacy objects, structures and gardens, without, however, taking them away from the pleasure of the visitors.

It is a difficult task—and as such an exciting one—to which all those who work at the villa and who are on the Board of the Society, first among which the staff, are devoted generously and without personal interest, in over seventy years of obscure but methodical work, carried out with loyalty and skill.

I wish here to thank all of the collaborators that made this publication possible, just as I wish to turn my thoughts to the memory of all of those, no longer here, who worked so that Villa Carlotta could continue to live for the present and future generations.

Giacomo Elias
President of the Villa Carlotta Society

Contents

From Villa Clerici to Villa Carlotta: the Origins

Pierre Paul Prud'hon, *Portrait of Count G.B. Sommariva*, Milan, Pinacoteca di Brera.

Princess Carlotta of Sassonia Meinengen.

The Clericis

The actual construction of the edifice, which goes back to the seventeenth century, is attributed to the Marquis Giorgio II Clerici. The founder of this famous family of Lake Como merchants was a man named Pietro Antonio Clerici, born in 1489 in Domaso, a small town in the territory of the ancient parish of Gravedona. The beginnings of the prospering commercial activity of the Clerici family are due to the son Cristoforo, whose textile business with several German cities led him to accumulate a considerable fortune, thereafter augmented by his son Giorgio, known as 'Giorgione.' The latter conquered a position of unquestionable importance in the silk industry, and accumulated so much wealth that he was able to diversify his work activity: in fact, from the year 1616 he became the financer of public funds, an extremely profitable investment through which he made a considerable amount of money. His immense wealth was inherited by his son Carlo who, through a series of authoritative public positions, greatly increased the family's social and economic prestige. When Carlo died, the Clerici wealth was divided between his two sons, Giorgio II and Giovanni Paolo. The first of the two, the legitimate heir, inherited the largest part of Carlo's possessions, that, in addition to the ancient estates of Cavenago and Cuggiono, included numerous possessions in the parish of Seveso, a series of properties distributed throughout the territories of Novara, Pavia, Alto Milanese and Lodigiano, Villa Simonetta in Milan, and two country residences in Niguarda and in Castelletto di Cuggiono. The exceptional political affirmation of Giorgio Clerici (1648-1736), crowned in 1717 by his nomination as President of the Senate, justifies his increasing desire to show off his prestige, also documented by the building of the villa of Tremezzo, the Clerici family's place of origin. Thus, it was a residence of representation, celebrating the Lake Como origins of the Clericis, probably erected during the last decade of the seventeenth century, or in association with the rise in the political career of the marquis. This explains the choice of the location, somewhat unsuited for building, because it is situated up against a slope on a very rugged piece of land, but one of great scenographic potential, fully exploited by the skillful use of the land's differences in levels. When Giorgio II died in 1736, and after the death of his son Carlo Francesco (1672-

Charles Boisfremont,
Boulangger, *Portrait
of Emilia Seillière
Sommariva.*

1722) and that of his grandson Carlo Giorgio (1696-1717), the very young great-grandson Antonio Giorgio (1715-1768) inherited the immense property of his great-grandfather. Devoted to a brilliant military career, as proven by the prestigious title of Knight of
the Golden Fleece, protector of the goods of the Holy Inquisition (1737), Milanese patrician (1739), grandee of Spain (1741), and General of the Artillery (1758), Antonio
Giorgio led a brilliant, worldly existence, dissipating the wealth he had inherited. The
object of his endless desire for ostentation was, in fact, the villa of Tremezzo: during his
intervention, revealed in the engravings by Dal Re and in a description by the Como historian Anton Gioseffo della Torre di Rezzonico, construction of the edifice was completed, and the entire complex of the garden was also finished, a garden that was in fact
characterized by spectacular scenographic inventions of typically eighteenth-century
taste. And during the period when it belonged to Claudia Biglia Clerici, the daughter of
Antonio Giorgio and the last of the Clericis to possess the building, the villa continued
to be a point of reference for the high life of the times, as revealed by the visit of the
Emperor Joseph II in 1769.

Sommariva

On 24 November 1801, Claudia Biglia Clerici, who did not have any children, sold Villa Clerici to Gian Battista Sommariva (1760-1826) for 72,500 lire. The sale included, in addition to the garden, the cottages, the vast piece of land overlooking the villa, transformed by the new owner, who was an impassioned botanist and vine-grower, into a panoramic 'English-style' park, the furniture and furnishings, as well, of which there is currently no trace. A native of Lodi and an illustrious representative of the emerging bourgeosie of the post-Revolutionary period, Sommariva considered this property to be the symbol of the redemption for his humble origins. A perfect incarnation of the self-made man *ante litteram*, he had been able to become a lawyer, and through a series of unprejudiced speculations that were not always legal, to accumulate an enormous wealth. This allowed him to acquire a position of importance also in the Milanese political environments, as revealed by his nomination as president of the Government Committe of the IInd Cisalpina Republic. The peak of his rise to power was his candidacy in 1802 as vice president of the Republic of Italy. Nonetheless, administrative politics that were without scruples had irremediably darkened his public image, so that, despite his links with the highest French political exponents, the much-desired job was entrusted to his adversary Francesco Melzi. Sommariva retired from public life, and went to live in his magnificent Parisian residence of rue Basse de Remparts, that along with the villa of Tremezzo constituted the location of his extraordinary antique and contemporary art collections. Once he had abandoned political life, he, in fact, reconverted his prestige, investing in works of art and patronizing the finest artists of the times (Canova, David, Thorvaldsen, Girodet all worked for this client), an activity that he carried out shrewdly, and that allowed him to recover his position in international high society, and his entrance amidst the most famous benefactors of the times. His nearly feverish need to accumulate works of art, dictated by a sincere love of art, was also met by the villa of Tremezzo: once all trace of the decorative Baroque had been removed, the villa took on the sole function of modern 'container' of the collections, nearly a residence-museum that was already at that time quite famous.

The Sassonia-Meiningen

When he died in 1838, with no children or siblings, Luigi Sommariva, the son of Giovanni Battista, divided the immense patrimony, including the precious art collections, amongst the widow Emilia Seillière Sommariva, numerous relatives, brothers and grandchildren of Gian Battista Sommariva and of his wife Giuseppina Verga. The Parisian art collections were auctioned off piece by piece in Paris, while the villa of Tremezzo was surrendered in 1834, along with its collections and the park, to Princess Marianne of the Netherlands, the wife of Prince Albert of Prussia, for 780,000 lire. On the occasion of the wedding in 1847 of the Grand Duke George II Sachsen Meiningen's daughter, the villa, given to the bride and groom and renamed Villa Carlotta, became the property of the German princes. Considering it a residence for strictly private use, and using it as a holiday location, they did not make any substantial changes in the furnishings or in the art collection. Nonetheless, they were devoted to the care and enrichment of the garden: this work is particularly due to Duke George I, a man of great culture and an impassioned botanist, who entrusted the redesigning of the park to a group of professionals, the authors of a typically Romantic transformation, that made of this location a unique example because of its exceptional variety of botanical species. When World War I broke out, Villa Carlotta was not subjected to sequester, as the property of enemy subjects usually was, rather it was placed under the management of a temporary administration. This situation continued until 1922, when the building risked being sold at an auction in favor of the Opera Nazionale Combattanti. Thanks to significant interventions by the lawyer Giuseppe Bianchini and the Rotary Club of Milano, the villa was fortunately entrusted in 1927 to the newly-founded Ente Morale Villa Carlotta, responsible for the management and the preservation of the edifice and the garden.

Villa Carlotta and the Lake: Tremezzina

A partial view of Tremezzina.

The 'outside' bank of the western branch of the Lario River, in the segment between Lenno and Grainte, derives its name 'Tremezzina' from the fisherman's hamlet known as 'Tramezzo' or 'Framezzo,' that developed between the Ancient Roman Via Regia (military route of the Imperial Age), to then become the 'Strada Regina,' and the slopes of Mount Crocione declining into the green morainic hills overlooking the water.

It is one of the most panoramic of areas: coming from the lake, one enjoys the large villas and the enchanting view of their carefully-groomed parks, the wharfs and the small harbors; arriving from the land one may glance over from the nearby peninsula of Balbaniello, just south of Lenno, as far as the more famous and suggestive spots of the opposite bank: from Bellagio, that with its sharp Punta Spartivento divaricates the lake into its well-known branches, as far as Varenna and Bellano; and the powerful and suggestive shape of the Grigne can be seen in the background.

The entire 'outside' coast is, on the other hand, of major historical and scenic importance because of the nearly uninterrupted succession of settlements, that from far back in time have influenced the coastal portion of the habitations. The region of the hilly and mountain hinterland has in the past undergone more modest and ephemeral construction work, of which hardly a trace remains today, because of the disappearance of the agricultural, sylvan, and pastoral acivities that had produced it.

What particularly distinguishes local building is the use of the gray 'Pietra di Moltrasio,' produced by the still-functioning quarries marking the coast.

The entire zone of the Lario, as in general that of the pre-Alpine lakes, between the eighteenth and the nineteenth centuries, was a necessary part of the itineraries of the Grand Tour, that long journey through Italy that represented the indispensable complement to a fine education. This is affirmed by numerous illustrious foreign citations (Goethe, Stendahl, Shelley), celebrating the beauty of these shores, at times choosing them as a back-drop to literary events, as did many Italian Romantic writers (Foscolo, Monti, Berchet, Cesare Cantù, Nievo, Fogazzaro, and, obviously, Manzoni).

What contributed to making those places uncomparable were the same elements that fascinate today's tourist: the mild climate, and the lush nature, the gracefulness of the coastal hamlets, and the extraordinary sequence of aristocratic villas that from the sixteenth century began to rise on the initiative of the Como nobility, and, more in general, of the Lombard aristocracy: the rustic beauty of the terracing cultivated with olives and citrus fruit was substituted by the austere beauty of 'Italian-style' gardens which were increasingly spectacular.

The brief coastal area of the Tremezzina is particularly rich in these patrician residences. At its threshold and extending into the lake is the Dosso di Lavedo or Balbaniello that hosts the villa of the same name, previously known as Arconati Visconti, and that today belongs to FAI; its original sixteenth-century nucleus was enlarged during the eighteenth century on the initiative of Cardinal Angelo Maria Durini. The two residential buildings, the portico, the oratory, and a small harbor, occupy the tip of the peninsula, entirely covered with the luxuriance of the park and the woods that define the western borders. The cardinal, a lover of music and letters, accomodated Parini there, while at a later date Silvio Pellico was present, often a guest at the anti-Hapsburgic meetings that the enlightened Milanese aristocracy also reunited on the banks of the Lario River. Once we have passed Lenno and Azzano, in the Bolvedro area, we encounter the monumental Villa Sola Cabiati, the central body of which dates back to the early eighteenth century. The front portion of the French garden maintains the original varyingly colored parterres decorated with areas of lawn, flower-beds, and arabesques of stone. Parini resided in this villa, too, for nine years a tutor in the Serbelloni residence, the family that had purchased the property. Also of interest is the adjacent Villa Albertoni, built in neoclassical style during the second half of the eighteenth century, and whose park maintains typical aspects of the 'Italian-style' garden, around the long flight of steps that rises as far as the villa, alongside the scenic elements typical of an 'English-style' garden.

Once we have passed Tremezzo and Villa Carlotta, we arrive at the area of Cadenabbia, so-called because of the old fisherman's inn 'Ca' del Nabia,' anticipating the future touristic vocation of the site, characterized by numerous hotels, among which the old and prestigious Grand Hotel Bellevue.

Just a bit further on, in another area of Griante, Maiolica, in a position higher up, one can view the Margherita-Ricordi Villa, built by Tito Ricordi, it seems, with the proceeds from the *Trovatore*, and in which Giuseppe Verdi resided for a long time as he composed the *Traviata*.

The hamlet of Cadenabbia with behind it the garden of Villa Carlotta.

The Garden at Villa Carlotta

Data on the life of Giorgio Clerici allow us to approximately date work to build the complex of the villa during the period that goes from 1684 to 1695. A further indication is provided us by a historian of Lake Maggiore, Agostino Cotta, who, in publishing a comment on a sixteenth- century text by Domenico Macaneo on the history of the Verbano in 1699, praised Isola Bella—that had been finished for nearly thirty years—hiding "the cedar forests of Tremezzo and…the 'Clerici' gardens." Once Giorgio Clerici died (1736), his heir and great-grandson, Antonio Giorgio, did none other than continue what had been initiated by his great-grandfather.

Another very important testimony is that of Marc'Antonio Dal Re who, devoting to Antonio Giorgio Clerici his second volume on the *Ville di Delizia* (1743), also printed numerous engravings of the villa of Tremezzo. These clearly reveal that the original project was based on eighteenth-century canons typical of the Lombard late Baroque, in which symmetry appears to be the norm most commonly followed. In fact, the various elements are specularly distributed around an axis that, from the gate, ideally crosses the fountain, the fortified terraces, the staircases, the entrance to the villa, the central atrium, and the back garden, ending there with a "very lovely Perspective of Mosaic," with many niches adorned with statues, in truth, never brought about and substituted by a simple retaining wall with a central aedicula, perhaps hosting a *Hercules Crushing Hydra*. The best descriptions of the property under Antonio Giorgio remain those of Dal Re and of the Como historian Anton Gioseffo della Torre di Rezzonico. Both sources express the magnificence of the garden. Dal Re describes the central nucleus: "One goes up to the Palazzo, walking up five comfortable Stairways, in the shape of two arms, with five stopping-places, the same number as the Terraces, all enriched with Espaliers of Citrus Fruit with many Vases…" Rezzonico adds other details describing a fishpond with a statue of Arion, the mythical lyre player and son of Neptune, saved by a dolphin. Rezzonico's mention of the central grotesque is interesting: "a grotto of various works…with latticed sides in the shape of a grille, with hidden spurts of water bursting from statues and from the mosaic pavement, as willed by the owner, splashing the unknowing spectators," just as had been taking place for some time in the grotto of Villa Visconti Borromeo Arese in Lainate.

Ruff, *Villa Sommariva,* engraving.

One of the engravings shows the arrangement of the areas closest to the villa, representing the two lateral, symmetrical gardens, each of which constituted by two square and two rectangular flower-beds.

It is not easy to get one's bearings in a maze of citations referred to elements that in part had been predicted, in part were only imagined, and only some of which were brought to term. As regards the floristic composition of the garden, the sources are silent, also because the first Clerici complex was nearly exclusively decorated with citrus plants that contributed to accentuating the classical flavor of the site. On the other hand, the architectural set-up of the garden must have considerably influenced the choice, perhaps reinforced by other climbing specimens—such as jasmines and roses—that for some time had been spreading on the lake.

The history of the lower terrace—the site of the fountain of Arion saved by the dolphin—and of the upper one, to the sides and north of the villa, is more tormented, both clearly tampered with during the Sommariva epoch and transformed into 'English-style' areas. In a map devised by the land-surveyor Giovanni Caprani in 1811, the terrace of the fountain appears to be constituted by flower-beds thickly covered with shrubs and herbaceous plants, surrounding winding paths that interest one another, just as in the upper terrace, to the west and to the east of the building, where subsequently a vast square was realized, today crowned by camellias that bloom in winter. Thus, it is evident that the Sassonia Meinengens were the ones to subsequently further re-elaborate in a late Romantic and eclectic key the terrace of the fountain, reintroducing the concept of symmetry by means of large hedges of camellias and cherry laurel, also found to the sides of the terrace. Despite this, one seems to be able to conclude that the primitive Clerici garden has remained nearly unmodified in its imposing 'Italian-style' scenographic composition, an authentic fulcrum around which the scenic-Romantic stratifications of the nineteenth century have been accumulated, resulting in an exceptional example of the successful fusion of two styles.

Giovanni Battista Sommariva made of Villa Clerici a center for the collection of splendid works of art, but he was equally interested in the garden, which was extended by the purchase of the surrounding land. From the letters that the lawyer from Lodi sent to his son Luigi between 1809 and 1825, it is observed that Sommariva, among other things an expert in agricultural sciences, was interested more in the cultivation of plants that produced food than in ornamental areas. With certainty we do know that Sommariva saw to introducing plants with a tall stalk that are typically Romantic. Nonetheless, the garden continued to privilege the cream of the entire property, that is, the Baroque terraces with their citrus ornaments. Sommariva's work at Tremezzo was depicted as a great landscaping operation, in which the old 'Italian-style' garden was harmoniously added to a multi-form agricultural context, made up of "olive trees and vineyards, small woodlands and fields, lawns and vegetable gardens," governed by five families of farmers.

As part of the work planned to connect the historical nucleus of the villa and the Baroque garden with the land used for agricultural purposes, the two paths to the west and to the east emerged, that were then used by the technicians of the Sassonia Meinengens as irregular axes for the constitution of a large Romantic garden, where the 'useful' plants were all substituted by flowering shrubs.

The Sommariva property lasted but a few years: the villa and its large park were sold in 1843 to Princess Marianne of the Netherlands, the wife of Prince Albert of Prussia, who in 1850 bestowed it on his daughter Charlotte, who married the Grand Duke George II Sachsen Meinengen. The latter, also with a passion for botany, immediately fell in love with the property of Tremezzo, and continued to embellish it even after the death of his wife. A first project of restructuring, in line with the Sommariva tradition, was intent on harmonizing the Baroque complex with the Romantic one, foreseeing the organization of a large scenic garden dependent on the long longitudinal paths that still characterize the complex, also by planting 'old' (citrus) and 'new' (oleanders, rhododendrons, and azaleas) species. Thus, areas of particular historical-scenic importance were exploited, such as the so-called 'Cascade of the Dwarfs,' or 'of the pygmies,' a steep slope entirely made up of cascades and grottoes to the west, or the old 'small valley of Rovedée,' today known as the 'Valley of the Ferns' bordering on the territory of Cadenabbia. A completely new accomplishment was the rock garden, for which plants from the gardens of the Meiningen court arrived, while the only loss was that of the 'Temple of Friendship,' situated by Sommariva at the high part of the park. Beginning with the Sassonia Meinengens, the garden and the park of Villa Carlotta have gradually been enriched with an increasing number of species, so that they are correctly identified as being an actual botanical garden. The high point of the fantastic Romantic season was achieved in around the years 1869-1870, when Villa Carlotta became famous for its unending richness, with plants arriving from the world over.

The passion for botanical exoticism was such that even the historical nucleus of the garden—the famous terraces at the front towards the lake—was nearly entirely covered with new plants: thickets of colored flowers, but above all shrubs, succulents and herbaceous perennials of strong impact.

The entire complex, expropriated by the Italian state in 1915, is now run by the Ente Morale Villa Carlotta, instituted in 1927, and at that time presided over by Count Giuseppe Bianchini. Not even during the course of the twentieth century has the original design of the villa and its park undergone substantial changes. And the current management, with its administrative and technical staff, has been capable of perfectly reconciling the care and enrichment of the botanical patrimony with the preservation of a historical-cultural reality that is more than three centuries old.

The Garden at Villa Carlotta: An Itinerary

The Sommariva Oratory.

A visit to the vast garden-park of Villa Carlotta can require from a few minutes to many hours, depending on the amount of time that one has available, and on the amount of curiosity that encourages one to obtain a more in-depth knowledge of a historical garden, that, in time, has nearly come to resemble a botanical garden. From this point of view, the case of Villa Carlotta seems to be an anomalous one, as, in general, the distinction between the two models of gardens is quite clear, at least in Italy. Nonetheless, the history of the location and its customs, even cultural ones, that have become stratified over the years, have led to a harmonious amalgam of the two souls, confirming a tendency that moreover already seemed well-initiated at the time of Gian Battista Sommariva. Thus, what might have seemed bizarre at the beginning, has gradually become a peculiarity: no visitor, today, is at all surprised to find alongside numerous species of ornamental value, a botanical identification—on the plaques fastened to a strong metal support—capable of providing succinct informative notes. The sobriety with which the signs have been located guarantees the most

absolute respect for the environment, so that it may justly be affirmed that the fusion between history, architecture, and botany has come about here without imbalance. The data provided by the plaques, nonetheless, however useful, particularly to those who for the first time find themselves in the vast plant kingdom, are necessarily brief, so that anyone who feels the need to obtain a more in-depth knowledge may profit from the guidance of an expert person or, if one is not available, a reading of this text. With a small amount of effort, we will thus be able to recognize the most interesting plant species in the garden, not only in terms of morphology, but also in relation to all of those curiosities that are triggered from the intertwining between the history of man and that of plants. We will thus have avoided accomplishing an epidermic, however healthy, 'dip into the greenery,' wandering here and there among the plants, but without ever arriving at truly understanding all of the messages that they, although speechless, are capable of transmitting by using other languages.

The itinerary—that will allow us to observe the single plants and at the same time savor the fascination of the arboreal masses and of the historically or scenically most valid locations—begins with a small entrance, alongside the Sommariva Oratory, that for some time now has substituted with its function that which was and is of the main gate. Once we have passed the ticket office, we walk down a short path that is flanked, in the direction of the lake, by a winding stone balustrade, topped with statues of mythological divinities, among which *Flora* and *Pomona*, of course, two ancient Italic goddesses symbolizing the cult of flowers and gardens. We immediately reach the base of the large scenographic composition, brought about by the rigorous scansion of the eighteenth century terraces, by the luminous main facade of the villa, and by the rich wealth of plants used to decorate and harmoniously fuse the stony and architectural elements. We are now in the lower part of the garden and, thus, glancing towards the lake, we try to imagine for an instant the scene that must have opened before the sight of he who, two or three centuries ago, landed here to be received and accomodated by the Clericis, the Sommarivas, or the Sassonia Meinengens. After going up a few steps, the imposing gate was opened before them, whose elegant frame was meant to deliberately reveal the magnificence of the property. Still today, the upper part of the gate is marked with a monogrammed 'C,' on the meaning of which opinions differ: there are some who relate it to the original property of the Clerici family, there are those who instead identify it as the symbol of Carlotta, the wife of the Grand Duke George II Sachsen Meinengen, who became the owner of the villa in 1850. Both hypotheses could be correct, but in favor of the second one is the dominating ducal crown, that cannot be attributed to the Clericis.

The entire circular flower-bed is centered on a splendid eighteenth-century fountain, which is also of evident mythological flavor, being dominated by the group

of statues of Arion saved by the dolphin. While the water of the small basin, in addition to goldfish, hosts plants of yellow and red nymphaea (*Nymphaea* cvs.) and at times blue water-hyacinths (*Eichhornia crassipes*), the surrounding border, with authentic French eighteenth-century spirit, is decorated with box-trees with small leaves that clearly contrast with the biennial spring (*Viola, Bellis, Myositis*) or annual summer (*Begonia, Tagetes, Salvia, Ageratum, Impatiens*) herbaceous plants. To the sides are thick hedges of cherry laurel (*Prunus laurocerasus*), laurel (*Laurus nobilis*) and camellia (*Camellia japonica*), accurately pruned 'a berceau' according to the age-old technique of topiary art. To break the geometrical schematisms of the composition, typical of the so-called 'Italian-style' garden, is the irregular arrangement of some of the plants, for example, on the right looking towards the villa, a group of palms that is well-acclimatized here. Hanging from one of their trunks is one of the many botanical plaques scattered throughout the garden, providing us with essential information. The name in Italian (Palma nana) is followed by the scientific de-

The 'C' monogram on the entrance gate.

The fountain of *Arion Saved by the Dolphin*.

rest at the end of their lesson in the open air.

If instead we are at the beginning of our visit, we face the hill towards the plane of the villa, going up the steps of the four terraces calmly, so as to be able to savor to the very end the beauties that surround us: the architectural and decorative elements, the radiant and quiet scenery of Lake Como, the numerous species that frame the picture. At the center of each dual stairway a 'grotesque' area opens up, decorated with sponge stones in which water has been running for many centuries, which is then collected in a basin below, where several acquatic plants are permanently located. In the case of the first terrace, there are two African species: trumpet lilies (*Zantedeschia aethiopica*), which are easily recognized because of their candid inflorescence shaped like a funnel, and a curious floating plant, *Aponogeton distachyus*, whose branching and white flowers give off a pleasant fragrance. Alongside the niche, two specimens of *Dasylirion acrotrichum* are in full view, close relatives of the agaves, and originating from Mexico. On their arborescent trunk leans a sphere of long leaves that are even up to 1 meter long, linear and rich in hooked thorns at the margins; when they are fully grown, these plants produce a robust inflorescence—made up of thousands of small flowers—that in nature may achieve even 4.5 meters in height. We then rise to the second 'grotesque' where, amidst small turtles and carps, each year large bundles of papyrus (*Cyperus papyrus*) grow, the plant from which the Egyptians obtained the material of the same name on which to write, that preceded paper: we will notice the abundant inflorescences constituted by umbels with 100-200 rays. Nearby, instead, lives an aromatic South American shrub lemon verbena (*Aloysia triphylla*), the wrinkled leaves of which give off a strong fragrance of citron or lemon. The upper terrace is then reached, by way of other staircases embellished with lateral

nomination in Latin (*Chamaerops humilis*, accompanied by an initial indicating the botanist who described the plant in a definitive manner: in this case, 'L' stands for Karl von Linné, or Linnaeus, Swedish, 1707-1778), followed by the family to which the species in question belongs in this case, *Palmae*, and, finally, the geographical area of origin (Mediterranean). From this group of dwarf palms it is easy to reach the construction located to the east of the formal 'Italian-style' garden and where picnics may be organized. It is sufficient to walk down the tunnel on the right of the palms to arrive at a path that, after grazing up against two beautiful beeches (*Fagus sylvatica* 'Pendula' and *F.s.* 'Purpurea Tricolor'), leads to a rose garden, alongside which rises a building where schoolchildren can

niches, containing vases with a very elegant Mexican shrub (*Russelia equisetiformis*), characterized by their weeping conveyance, with leaves in the shape of scales and numerous red flowers that also hang. The terrace that we now reach has a sufficiently wide surface, so that the annual and biennial herbaceous plants can be arranged in two lateral flower-beds, which precede the two large and renowned tunnels of citruses. Continuing and further developing a tradition that by now counts more than three centuries—when the primitive Clerici garden was defined by Cotta a 'cedar forest'—the gardeners of Villa Carlotta are passionately and with great technical ability devoted to the cultivation of citruses in the ground, that at this latitude certainly represents a rare event. In this case, moreover, it must be observed that the collection is qualitatively considerable, as, alongside the more common lemons (*Citrus limon*) and the bitter oranges (*C. aurantium*), we are awaited here by a succession of hybrids of various species,

but also by sweet oranges (*C. sinensis*), tangerines (*C. reticulata*), myrtle-leaved organges (*C. myrtifolia*), grapefruits (*C. x paradisi*), mandarine oranges (*C. unshiu*), bergamots (*C. bergamia*) and kumquats (*Fortunella margarita*). The care taken for the continuous renewal of hybrids and species and for their preservation in the first place calls for a location that is covered in winter—made up of two tunnels with a permanent structure in wood and mobile covering in plastic—that guarantees a temperature of not less than 4-5° C. Plant protection is frequent and routine, thus combatting the different diseases that may strike these kinds of plants. At the end of the western tunnel, another fruit shrub, but one that pertains to the family of the *Myrtaceae*, is leaned up against the structure of the citruses, as if it were in search of protection. Its vulgar name in Portuguese is Feijoa (*Acca sellowiana*), an evergreen species of Brasilian and Uruguayan origin, introduced in Europe in 1819. It is quite rare in parks and it is more frequent in botan-

First terrace.

The tunnel of citrus plants.

ical gardens, because the interest that it arouses above all resides in its fruit, very sweet in flavor if the summer sun has ripened it sufficiently, halfway between the fig and the pineapple. It must be added that its flowers are also very attractive, with their four curving petals of whitish red color, and that they deserve more.

We continue in our ascent towards the main building, also taking a glance at the numerous roses that decorate the walls supporting the stairways. In many cases, these are very old specimens that have with dignity survived over the years, but the most beautiful and spectacular rose is the 'Mermaid,' a hybrid between a *Rosa bracteata* and a tea rose, constituted in 1918—the fascination of which resides not only in its growth, that may even achieve 10 m in length, but above all in the large yellow bunch-like flowers, slightly fragrant and with a simple corolla, that continue to bloom until late au-

The succession of terraces from the villa level.

Suggestive view of Lake Como.

'Mermaid' rose.

The last terrace on the villa level.

of *Bougainvillea* and *Brugmansia* (at one time part of the genus *Datura*), in addition to an attractive creeping or hanging shrub of South African origin, *Plumbago auriculata*, with its very rich blue masses of flowers. Between the niches, the spaces are entirely covered with an evergreen creeping plant of particular interest, because of the very fragrant flowering that lasts for even longer than a month: it is the false jasmine (*Trachelospermum jasminoides*), originating from China. The long retaining walls that extend to the sides of the villa are, in turn, covered with other creeping plants, this time more rustic ones, such as roses, clematis (*Clematis*) and wisteria (*Wisteria sinensis*).

The Camellias

After completing the visit inside the villa, we resume our itinerary in the garden exiting from the Sala dei Marmi and, therefore, from the back entrance, that faces onto the niche that perhaps at one time held a statue of Hercules. Today, the sponge niche is nearly entirely covered with a graceful spontaneous fern, the maidenhair fern (*Adiantum capillus-veneris*), its soft fronds falling under the constant trickle of water. To the sides, left and right, tall and dark evergreen hedges pruned in a regular and geometrical fashion offer us the opportunity to reflect on one of the species that has adapted best to the environment of Villa Carlotta: camellias. A first blooming of these plants in Italy was observed in the gardens of the Reggia di Caserta, towards the year 1760, but an actual production of specimens on a large scale began around the end of the eighteenth century, in the Florentine greenhouses of Count Leopoldo Galli (1794) and in Milan, in those of the physician Luigi Sacco, the famous divulger of the vaccine against smallpox. Of the 267 species found around the world, unquestionably the most important is the *Camellia japonicam* from which the first cultivators and nurserymen had departed, thanks to the versatility of the plant, that

tumn. Our difficult but pleasant ascent finally ends at the lower level of the villa, where we cannot but turn in the direction of the lake, perhaps leaning up against the last balustrade, surrounded by vases of geraniums (*Pelargonium*), by beautiful specimens of hibiscus (*Hibiscus rosa-sinensis*) and by multicolored tufts of a happy South African herbaceous plant (*Nemesia strumosa*). We once again glance at the underlying terraces and, beyond the elegant gate, at the shining lake and at the horizon, with the tip of Bellagio and the luminous Villa Melzi that calls us from afar. Before crossing the threshold of the historical building to visit the splendid rooms and the works of art (see Part I), it is worth considering the vegetational decoration that characterizes the large niches and the arches underlying the villa. Under their shelter are cultivated non-rustic species, such as some hybrids

allowed for it to give life to more than 2,000 varieties. Its spontaneous form, anything but ostentatious, is demonstrated by its very simple red corollas with only five petals, but the ability of those with a passion for the flower has drawn marvelous 'cultivar,' particularly by stimulating the plant and transforming some of its stamens into petals, resulting in many forms with semi-double or double flowers, and above all with many-colored or variegated corollas. If we judge by the size achieved by the numerous specimens that we observe in this northern courtyard, it seems that we may conclude that the use of the camellia in Villa Carlotta goes back a long time, even if the documentation does not provide us with a precise date: it is a fact, however, that among the different varieties here rooted, it is easy to find several which have fallen into disuse over the years. Because of

The high hedges of camellias to the sides of Hercules' niche.

Camellia japonica 'Lavinia Maggi'.

A winter camellia:
Camellia sasanqua
'Jean May'.

ferred to the species *Camellia sasanqua*, Japanese, others instead to the hybrid *Camellia* x *hiemalis*, a cross between the *C. japonica* and the *C. sasanqua*. What is particular about these shrubs is that in addition to being unusually low if compared to other camellias, they bloom many months before, from October to January, but with flowers of modest size.

Greenhouse Plants

If we trace back on our steps, we once again return to the main path that goes east, trimmed with evergreen borders of *Ophiopogon japonicus*—commonly known as 'lily of the valley'—a Japanese herbaceous plant that since the nineteenth century has been used in European gardens to border pedestrian routes or to decorate areas under large trees. Suddenly, it is nearly dark, although it is still daytime: in fact, to the left, high hedges of camellias continue, while to the right, a thick wall of evergreens and conifers separates us from the blinding light of the lake. In this zone, on both sides, each year the gardeners of the villa usually situate a rich series of plants in vases, planting them, after having kept them in greenhouses during the winter months. They are all exotic species, not very rustic and decidedly delicate, that attract our attention because of their unusual, even bizarre shapes, as well as their spectacular flowering. To the right we admire large tufts of tropical ferns (*Platycerium*), purposefully fastened to the trunk of a Scotch pine (*Pinus sylvestris*) to recall that we are dealing with epiphytes, that is, plants that in nature survive by hanging from other specimens, without actually being parasites. In fact, they are provided with roots and leaves that have a special structure, capable of absorbing water from the atmosphere, nutritionally satisfied by the mineral dust deposited at their bases. On the ground, instead, orchids prevail, pertaining to the *Sobraliam Cymbidium*, *Oncidium*, *Vanda* and *Stanhopea* genuses: the latter, of South American origin, have

their stupefying variety, we could spend hours just admiring the different corollas that, nearly a reflex action, we are used to sniffing in the vain search for a fragrance that they usually do not have: very few camellias have a fragrance, and these do not include the most common types, such as *C. japonica* and *C. reticulata*.

Our itinerary now tells us to turn east, so that behind the oriental side of the villa, we see a vast space as it opens up, from which it is once again possible to admire the lake scenery. A bit off-center, a solitary specimen of bay laurel (*Laurus nobilis*) catches the eye, one of the most common Mediterranean evergreen plants—well-known in the kitchen— while all around, in a semi-circle, a series of evergreens develops, among which of particular interest is a beautiful group of hybrids of winter camellias, some re-

large flowers that give off a delightful fragrance. Alongside them temporarily located is a specimen of *Calliandra tweedii*, a Brasilian leguminous plant, the common name of which in English sounds like 'powder puff,' alluding to the flowers that have numerous filaments of a vivacious flaming red color, which are not unlike those of the more famous *Albizia julibrissin*. If we instead turn to the left, we see a mass of another species that we have already encountered inside an apartment, like the Asiatic Ficus (*F. elastica* and *F. benjamina*), the South African *Strelitzia reginae* and *S. alba* the flowers of which recall a bird in flight, the South America *Monstera deliciosa*, the ostentatious *Acalypha wilkesiana* originally of the Pacific Islands, the palms of the *Howea* genuses (*H. forsteriana*, also known as Kentia) and *Chamaedorea* (the Guatemalan *C. elegans* one of the most commonly cultivated house palms). And there are other various species of the *genera Philodendron, Pothos, Dracaena, Asplenium, Justicia* (previously known as *Beloperone*), *Polypodium*, in addition to numerous *Bromeliaceae*, the family that also includes the pineapple and the epiphyte *Tillandsia*. It resembles an assembly of plants coming from the world over, gathered here to pay cosmopolitan homage to one of the most 'romantic' sites in the garden. Behind them, in fact, we may observe a structural decorative element typical of the nineteenth century garden, the so-called 'grotto,' a small area dug at the base of a mountain and entirely lined inside with 'sponge' rocks, that clearly fit the taste of the days of the Sassonia Meinengens or perhaps even of Sommariva. In essence, the building of an artificial grotto—even if it had previously been used in the old secret garden of the sixteenth-seventeenth centuries—in the nineteenth century constituted one of the most effective stratagems to make explicit an important principle of the so-called 'English-style' garden, consisting in creating the idea of a 'surprise' for the visitor, thanks also to the artful return to na-

Justicia brandegeana, previously know as *Beloperone*.

ture: "grottoes," the French landscapist Edouard André writes in 1879, "that at one time served as homes for men, are today a simple curiosity, they are attractive objects in parks and gardens, as long as they maintain a natural appearance."

The Theatre of Greenery

The path now continues straight and, after a few meters, it is more luminous, because the evergreen mass thins out, allowing the light from part of the lake to filter in. If we make an effort to look to the left, however, we will see an unexpected vision, offered by a surprising scenographic perspective exclusively brought about by plant material: a grassy and winding route that rises on the slopes of the mountain, bordered on the sides by wings of shrubs, in splendid florescence between April and May. The perspective vanishing point is constituted

The Theater of
Greenery.

by a back-drop of high conifers (*Pinus nigra* and *Cedrus atlantica*) which our eyes are nearly forced to look at under the guidance of the shrubs arranged in a spherical mass, with no geometrical rigor and with apparent chanciness. It is an authentic modern 'theater of greenery,' the fascination of which cannot be overlooked, beginning with the bride and groom that have their picture taken here after the wedding ceremony. In addition to the grassy carpet, a single plant is queen here: the azalea, the botanical glory—together with the camellia—for which the garden of Villa Carlotta is famous. And the rhododendrons, another proud element of this enchanting garden, can they perhaps be forgotten? Certainly not, but we must immediately add that for botanists, there is not much of a dif-

Amomyrtus luma
previously knows as
Myrtus luma.

A specimen of Chinese rice paper (*Tetrapanax papyrifer*).

ference between azaleas and rhododendrons, in scientific terms. Both are part of the same genus *Rhododendron*, even if three sub-genera have been identified, of which one dedicated to 'azaleas' alone. From a practical and floricultural point of view, a distinction continues to be considered valid, that on a scientific level, nonetheless, has no basis. It may only be affirmed in general that azaleas—generally, but not always, as stated here—are deciduous in the winter months, while rhododendrons are prevalently evergreens; furthermore, the former are commonly smaller in size, in terms of flowers and leaves, as compared to actual rhododendrons. What is certain is that the shrubs that we are now admiring, in this unusual 'theater of greenery' all pertain to the sub-genus *Azalea*, and, in particular, they have been chosen in a careful and balanced manner in relation to graded florescence and chromatic contrasts.

It is difficult to depart from this scene of nearly pastoral flavor, but there is still much to be seen, and it is best now to stop and look at the vast lawn-like flowerbed that extends southward, slightly sloping, like a stage opening onto the lake. Let us abandon for a while the main path and take a secondary one that, immediately to the right, descends in steps in a

downwards direction. Leaving to the left an old yew (*Taxus baccata*), we now proceed east, walking along a border mixed with trees and shrubs of great botanical interest. In succession, we will observe: a specimen of *Thujopsis dolabrata* 'Variegata,' a Japanese conifer that resembles a thuja, but the leaves of which are larger and flatter; another old *Araucaria cunninghamii*, Australian, with typical tufts of small green branches on the tips of its main naked branches; two magnolias, one an evergreen (*Magnolia grandiflora*) and one deciduous (*Magnolia* x *soulangiana*); several specimens of myrtle (*Myrtus communis*); an evergreen shrub of the Mediterranean with aromatic leaves and small bluish fruit; another myrtle plant (*Myrtus luma*, today known as *Amomyrtus luma*), that comes from Chile and has a very beautiful trunk with large spots the color of coppered ochre. The path begins to turn towards the north in proximity of a group of Australian eucalyptuses of two species: *Eucalyptus viminalis*, majestic, its trunk smooth and nearly white, and *E. globulus*, its leaves in the shape of a crescent, and sea-green fruit, strongly aromatic. It is worth recalling that the genus *Eucalyptus* includes the highest trees in all of the vegetable kingdom, surpassing 155 m with the species *E. amygdalina*.

View of the Rock Garden.

View of the Rock Garden.

The Palms

To return to the main path, we continue to walk along the border of the large lawn-like flower-bed on our left, that at this oriental end hosts a thick group of exotic palms: two species of *Phoenix*— the same genus as the date palm—that is, *P. canariensis*, originally of the Canary Islands, with a shorter and thicker trunk, and *P. sylvestris*, Indian, which is thinner and taller, and that has leaves that reach a length of 4.5 m; the Californian *Washingtonia filifera*, which is 10 meters tall and characterized by a stalk covered with the residues of dry leaves that have now fallen; the Guadalupe palm (*Erythea*, today also known as *Brahea, edulis*), with an irregularly angular trunk the leafstalks of which go up to 1.5 m in length, with leaves that may be up to 2 m wide; the 'fan palm' (*Rhapis flabelliformis*), of Chinese-Japanese origin, also known as the 'dwarf fan palm' or 'lady palm,' because of its modest height, with stalks that are so subtle that they deceive anyone observing it in its natural formation, possibly exchanging it for a reed; finally, the previously known palm of the Mediter-

ranean (*Chamaerops humilis*) and the palm most commonly present in our gardens (*Trachycarpus fortunei*), of Chinese origin, that adapts to our climates to the point that in some cases it actually overruns the area in which it is situated. But the palm-grove of Villa Carlotta holds a few more surprises, constituted by species pertaining to other families, such as a pair of agaves native of New Zealand (*Cordyline australis*), having delightfully fragrant flowers and long and elegant leaves, that in some varieties are purple-prune in color. Nearby, an *Araliaceae* known as 'Chinese rice paper' (*Tetrapanax papyrifer*) seems to want to compete with the palms, its upper leaves up to half a meter in width: its medulla is used in China to produce rice paper. Another South American species, that shows itself off in virtue of its enormous leaves, the diameter of which may even exceed 2 m, is the *Gunnera manicata*, a herbaceous plant with no stalk, the cultivation of which requires considerably humid ground. As we gradually once again come close to the 'Theater of Greenery,' from which we had departed, the orna-

mentation of the large lawn-like flower-beds gradually tapers off into a simple presence of perennial herbaceous plants, such as asters (*Aster*) and then *Hemerocallism*, *Crinum* and *Iris*, followed, not much farther away, by a group of Japanese bananas (*Muso basjoo*), cultivated by us only for ornamental reasons, because of their long and fringed leaves. Let us not fool ourselves into thinking that we can pick its fruit, even if we saw some, as it would not exceed a length of 6 cm and at any rate cannot ripen here.

The Rock Garden

At this point we are able to satisfy a curiosity that has been gnawing at us since we left the azaleas of the 'theater' (that the gardeners have always called 'Zoca'), glimpsing to the right an area of multicolored flowering, that from the underlying border of conifers and myrtles, as well, had attracted our attention. We immediately realize that it is a rock garden with a specific plant arrangement, because it is constituted by an upper crown of shrubs of excellent ornamental impact, overshadowing a mosaic of perennial herba-

ceous plants that bloom in the spring, and annual and biennial herbaceous plants that prevalently bloom in the summer. Among the shrubs we discern a 'Fog tree' (*Cotinus coggyria* 'Royal Purple'), a variety with brownish-purple leaves of a Eurasiatic species, with large and loose terminal panicles of small flowers that are so evanescent that they resemble drops of fog; a hybrid of St.-John's-wort for the garden (*Hypericum* x *moserianum*) with large yellow flowers; a shrub-like potentilla (*Potentilla fruticosa*), that in nature is expressed in many sub-species and varieties from which horticulturists have taken countless varieties with hundreds of different colors; a *Ceanothus* x *delilianus* 'Gloire de Versailles,' a hybrid between two species of a genus of North African shrubs, that are distinguished for the very abundant mass of small flowers that are usually light blue gathered in cymes similar to umbels; a Spirea (*Spiraea japonica* 'Bumalda'), a short shrub with large inflorescences that are scarlet red in color and that bloom all summer long; and then much less rustic plants, such as the *Fuchsia*, with its magnificent hanging flowers,

Aubrieta, a carpet-like perennial plant.

Succulent plants in the Rock Garden.

forces us to remain a few minutes, almost as if we did not want to leave such a scene. If our visit takes place in spring, our careful observation takes in an unusual scene occurring at a higher level, where the trunk and the primary branches of a tall black pine (*Pinus nigra*) are clasped by the coils of a very old specimen of wisteria (*Wisteria sinensis*), nearly a request for support and shelter, so that from afar anyone can admire the blue bunches in bloom of one of the most beautiful creeping plants to exist in nature. Originally from China, but cultivated in Europe since 1825, this species is part of a genus that is not particularly vast. All ten of the species up to the present acknowledged have typical twining stems, that in some cases become actual trunks, even tens of meters tall; their diameter may achieve 80 cm, while the bark that is grayish in color is cracked, so that it gives the whole plant the appearance of being 'old,' even when it is really quite young . It is interesting to observe the direction in which the stalks of the different types of wisteria are entangled: a first group, among which the Japanese *W. Floribunda*, rises upwards with a 'clockwise' movement—that is, from left to right— while a second group, guided by the Chinese *W. Sinensis*, has instead chosen the opposite direction of the hands of a clock, rising, that is, from right to left. The conifer that our wisteria asks protection of, the black pine, is frequently called 'Austrian pine,' amd it is a conifer of dark and imposing aspect that is distinguished from the similar Scotch pine that we encountered near the 'grotto' because it has longer needles. This pine is one of the most suited for the formation of shelter, and the protection of the more delicate trees; furthermore, good pulp may be obtained with its wood.

and the tropical *Lantana,* with its hemispherical heads with corollas that range from yellow, to red, to orange. A pair of shrubs closer to our latitudes complete the picture, but it is not for this reason that they are less fascinating: a rockrose (*Cistus albidus*)—with small leaves of modest dimension and flowers with round and silky petals—and a group of lavenders (*Lavandula angustifolia*), with their fragrant dark and light blue spikes. This entire group of shrubs of varying origin accompanies a not less nourished series of spring perennial herbaceous plants (white *Iberis,* purplish *Aubrieta,* silver *Cerastium* and yellow *Alyssum*), that in the summer leave a place for other plants, this time annuals or biennials, that are again very colorful (*Tagates, Impatiens, Begonia, Ageratum...*). From all of this gushes forth a particular and blinding fascination, that attracts us and nearly

If we now look right, following the rock garden, our attention will be gained by several specimens of *Dasylirion acrotrichum,* and above all by a sort of palm, that we will discover instead belongs to the family of the *Cycadaceae,* a

The Valley of Ferns.

gymnosperm of very ancient origins, present on the Earth from the end of the Carboniferous period. It is a *Cycas revoluta*, Japanese in origin, with leaves that may even be 1.5 m long, smooth, shiny, and divided into linear-lanceolate small leaves, praised for its ornamental conveyance, even if in its native land its long red seeds are also appreciated, to be eaten cooked or even raw. Here it is in the company of other species that are completely different in appearance and origin. Truly unusual, a United States palm from the sub-tropical region (*Sabal palmetto*), that is, however, quite rustic, and that can be cultivated even at this latitude; in its native country its trunk grows to 30 m, with a diameter of 60 cm, but here it is more modest in size, continuing, however, to show its very beautiful and large whitish-green fronds, that may even be 2 m long. It is kept company by a specimen of *Callistemon coccineus*—of Australian origin, and a relative of the myrtle, with curious summer spikes of red flowers that resemble tube-brushes used to clean bottles—and a 'Coral tree' (*Erythrina crista-galli*), from South America, with ostentatious red-scarlet flowers, that are single or grouped in large terminal racemes, not always easy to acclimatize in areas that are not tropical.

The rock garden does not end here, because more to the east a second area extends—characterized by large pockets or niches, dug into rugged ground and separated from one another by rocks and stones—capable of accomodating a considerable number of cactuses, that are arranged here during the good season, to be taken back to the greenhouse when it begins to get cold. It is a wonderful assortment of succulents, and not a collection limited to just one type, containing

Tulip tree (*Liriodendron tulipifera*).

phological features that liken it, although only on the outside, to a *Cactaceae*: with its very spiny shrubs, it is totally without leaves, as those in the shape of a cross that we observe are only an extension of its small branches. Finally, the last partner of the cactuses is the *Yucca recurvifolia* 'Variegata,' a plant from the United States that is also of the *Agavaceae* family, that is, however, a shrub with a woody stalk and long evergreen leaves in the shape of a sword, and that prickle at the top. Finally, and how they got here we do not know, two fruit trees: a pomegranate (*Punica granatum*) with 'beautiful vermillion flowers,' and very elegant leaves, alongside a specimen of an avocado (*Persea americana*), with evergreen ovate-elliptical leaves that are also a bit leathery, that unfortunately in this climate is not capable of producing its famous fruit (fleshy drupe) to be eaten as a dessert, in frozen creams, or as an appetizer.

The Valley of the Ferns

After this long stop, if we have had the patience to examine bit by bit each plant of the rock garden and its cornice, we proceed along the main path and—once we have surpassed to the left a fork leading upwards, introduced by a large wild linden (*Tilio cordata*)—we find ourselves on a terrace with a view that resembles a small stage of a theater turned towards a back-drop that is totally green. Known as the 'Valley of the Ferns' the scene that we now have before us is none other than a wide gorge with flanks that are not too steep, that is situated to the sides of a brook that acts as a confine between the territory of Tremezzo, to the left, and that of Cadenabbia, to the right. The skillful hand of the landscaper has known how to transform a common natural ravine—known in dialect as 'valletta di Rovedée'—into a scenographically constructed environment, with the purpose of amazing the visitor, by means of the calibrated addition of several species of trees (lindens and plane-trees), but

several species pertaining to about fifteen different genera. Thus, we go from the more common *Opuntia, Aloe, Agave, Sedum* and *Euphorbia,* to the less known *Cereus, Mammillaria, Gasteria, Echeveria, Kalanchoe, Kleinia, Epiphyllum, Zygocactus,* not to mention the famous 'nun's cushion' (*Echinocactus grusonii*), a *Cactaceae* on the sharp and barbed spines of which no one would like to be seated. Although they do not belong to the category of the succulent, other plants are an equally appreciated part of this company, such as the bizarre and nearly monstruous *Encephalartos horridus,* from South Africa, of the *Zamiaceae* family, a close relative of the *Cycas,* and, similarly, originating in the faraway Paleozoic era, and surving until the present, so that it is considered an authentic 'living fossil.' *The Colletia cruciata,* too, a South American plant, has mor-

above all plants extraneous to the spontaneous flora of this area. In fact, in addition to a reinforcement of the shrubbery, obtained by adding evergreens such as *Prunus laurocerasus* and *Aucuba japonica*, each spring the scene is enriched by the planting of large vases of arborescent and palmiform ferns originating from Australia, such as *Dicksonia antarctica* and *Alsophila* (today known as *Cyathea*) *australis*. The spectacle, for one observing from the belvedere, is certainly one of great effect, so that one truly appreciates the efforts not only of the person who takes on the task of transporting and planting these plants twice yearly, but also the care that these plants require in the greenhouse. Without moving too far from this location, it is enough to just turn to see, on the other side of the path, a truly majestic tree trunk. If we look upwards, we realize that we are being sheltered by widely spherical foliage, with robust and polished branches, covered with a mass of leaves that are light green and of a strange trapezoidal shape. It is a 'tulip tree' (*Liriodendron tulipifera*), a spontaneous species that grows in the Eastern United States—from Massachusetts as far as Florida—where it reaches the maximum height of 60 m. Its scientific Latin denomination indicates that this tree is 'a lily-tree that carries tulips,' to recall the appearance of its flowers, that are greenish-yellow in color. The decorative effectiveness of this species, nonetheless, certainly resides in its leafage, elegant in shape, lively under the games played by the sun and wind, and attractive in color, so that in spring and in summer as well as in autumn, its intense yellow is the most beautiful among all of the deciduous trees.

The Azaleas

From this point onwards, if our visit takes place in April-May, we must be ready to delve into an authentic sea of multicolored azaleas, that with high rounded cushions give shape to the lateral walls. The effect is undoubtedly unique, be-

cause of the extraordinary chromatic variety expressed by these generous decorative plants, and because of the size reached by the shrubs, that are so compact and thick that we cannot at all discern their woody part: they seem to be made solely with flowers and leaves suspended in the air. Here it is truly possible to tangibly verify the ability of he who, from the landscapers of the Sassonia Meinengen era to today's gardeners, has known how to accomplish a route in bloom of this scope, interpreting in a modern key the objectives and the techniques of age-old topiary art. If in the classical Italian garden pruning with a specific shape was exclusively carried out on evergreen species (for example, box-tree and laurel), here even more surprising effects have been obtained, obviously without respecting the rigid geometrical rules of the past. If we wish to observe

The long path bordered by azaleas of many colors.

The romantic gazebo that opens onto Lake Como.

the scene with greater comfort, we take a very short path to the right, that in a few meters leads to a gazebo of obvious Romantic flavor: from this location it will seem to us that we cannot have any other vision of the world except for that made of waves of azaleas, of walls of arboreal rhododendrons and of lake water. The fusion between plant architecture and natural scenery is immediate here, corroborated by a delightful fragrance that the spring sun is able to draw forth from the flowers and the leaves. Before going back, we will appreciate the grace-fulness of the same structure in the wrought iron of the gazebo, along which run the thin and fragile stems of two creeping plants that bloom for a long time: *Solanum jasminoides* and *Solanum crispum* 'Glasnevin,' both of which are South American.

Having ended our journey into this ine-briating world, we go back to the main path—abandoned to go down to the gazebo—and, if we are so fascinated by the azaleas to want to admire them one by one—we continue on the right, until we arrive at a small space in which a sort

of sarcophagus in Roman style dominates, today used as a planter. The path then rises bending to the left: after a few steps, to the right, at the end of a very short fenced road, we see a gigantic specimen of a Chinese 'False camphor tree' (*Cinnamomum glanduliferum*), one of the most fascinating evergreen trees of the entire garden. Although it is confined to a corner that is not fitting of its size, the 'camphor tree' appears in all of its majesty, unfolding the virtues that nature has assigned this genus of tree of the *Lauraceae* family, therefore also of the laurel. It is 25 m tall, with a smooth trunk when it is young, to then become increasingly wrinkled; the tree—even in the species most suited for the extraction of camphor, *C. camphora*, very similar to a *C. glanduliferum*—is a splendid ornamental plant, particularly because of its leaves, which are very elegant, fragrant and of a lovely tender green.

Just a bit further on, again to the right, is the lovely trunk furrowed by long suberose ribs and cracks of a calocedrus *(Calocedrus decurrens)*, a North American *Cupressaceae* that resembles a tuja, although with considerably different fruit, which is oblong and not spherical. It is a conifer of great effect, with a straight trunk and thick and compact leafage, which at times gives off a vague odor of incense; its height, that on the mountains of Oregon and California reaches 45 m, stops here at 25-27 m, but its conveyance, at the same time vigorous and graceful, suggests a more frequent use in parks and gardens, after having adequately calculated its living space. The suggestion is now to consider the calocedrus as a point of reference and, instead returning almost as far back as the 'Valley of the Ferns,' at the onset of the very long path of azaleas, to enter into the path that gently rises upwards, in an eastern direction. Immediately at the beginning, on the left, a second rock garden begins, smaller than the previous one, overshadowed by the dark foliage of a yew (*Taxus baccata*). Three

Masses of azaleas towards the Strada Regina.

False Chinese camphor (*Cinnamomum glanduliferum*).

The second Rock Garden.

more conifers, but smaller in size, are distributed amidst the shrubs and the flowering herbaceous plants: a second yew with a dwarf-like conveyance (*Taxus baccata* 'Cavendishii'), a *Chamaecyparis obtusa* 'Nana Gracilis,' a small Canadian fir with thin leaves (*Picea glauca* var. *albertiana* 'Conica'). Apart from the usual spring and summer herbaceous plants, it is interesting here to observe some flowering shrubs: a Central American composite (*Eupatorium ligustrinum*) with corymbs measuring a diameter of 20 cm; a 'Mexican orange' (*Choisya ternata*), with beautiful digitate and shiny leaves and rich inflorescences of white and fragrant flowers; a *Cuphea ignea*, also Mexican, that the English call 'cigar flower,' because of the cylindrical shape of its corolla, scarlet in color with white margins; groups of fuchsias and other species already encountered, such as the

Plumbago auriculata, Colletia cruciata and *Hypericum* x *moserianum*. To all of these species are added shrubs with ornamental leaves or fruits: *Sarcococca saligna*, originally from the Himalayas, an evergreen and a relative of the box-tree, with long strictly lanceolate leaves, a lovely pale green in color, also suited for hedges, the evergreen *Cotoneaster franchetti*, Chinese in origin, with small, graceful, oval leaves, topped by orange-scarlet fruits.

The Wood of the Rhododendrons

Further along, to the right, a narrow and winding path returns to gently run downwards, leading us into another historical location of the garden of Villa Carlotta, the so-called 'Wood of the Rhododendrons.' The expression used to name this location is not redundant or poetic, because we immediately realize that, in

truth, an unknown landscaper from the past (probably dating back to the times of the Sassonia Meinengens) with a single species of rhododendron (*Rhododendron arboreum*) was able to recreate, on the banks of the Lario River, a scene that can only be equalled on the Himalayan Mountains. The results of that project is now before our eyes, happily amazed in confirming how the skill and the taste of a garden planner have been able to so perfectly reproduce an environment that is so distant—geographically and climatically, as well as in terms of the vegetational view—from that Insubric Lake Como. The arboreal rhododendron is spontaneous, particularly with its numerous sub-species and natural varieties, not only on the Himalayas, but also in the territories that go from China to Thailand, as well as in India and Sri Lanka. Characterized by a thick trunk with no branches in its lower part, 30-60 cm in diameter and from 1 to 15 m in height (up to a maximum of 19 m), this species is an actual tree, with lanceolate or oblong leaves and racemose embel inflorescences with 15-20 flowers, a beautiful crimson-red in color in the typical species, or rosy or even white in some of the sub-species. At its spontaneous state, it can survive mixed in with oaks, pines, and other conifers, or it can develop pure formations, at an altitude that ranges from 1,200 to 3,400 m. Discovered in 1796, it was introduced at the beginning of the nineteenth century in Europe, where it bloomed for the first time in 1825 in England. Its florescence takes place quite early, so that even in Tremezzo, in recent years, it has even taken place during the month of March. The woods in which we now find ourselves, despite the inevitable damage caused by the passing of time, is

The Wood of the Rhododendrons.

Pinus montezumae with very long needles.

The vast lawn crowned by trees and flowering shrubs.

still in good general condition, but some of the symptoms of the fungi diseases have forced the Management of the Villa to arrange a second area, more to the north, in which to recreate a similar site, that may, if need be, act as a substitute in a perhaps near future. It will not be an easy task, nor will it be a brief one, as the formation of a 'pure' woods requires years of work and accurate planning, and one must not give in to the temptation to add other species, that could denaturalize the original design. Still today, in fact, it is possible to observe that, in the shade of the arboreal rhododendrons of this wood, other plants do not thrive, except for the lush tufts of a perennial and very rustic evergreen herbaceous plant (*Aspidistra elatior*), a specimen of *Fatsia japonica* and several groups of hydrangeas.

The path that crosses the wood, sinuous

and irregular, finally more or less leads to the area in which we had left the calocedrus (*C. decurrencs*), so that it will not be difficult to return to the route along the path that now rises with sharp curves until it ends, in turn, in another curvilinear path that is farther above. The scene here is much wider, with a large lawn to the left dotted with trees and shrubs of different sizes and nature. At first we encounter several large specimens of *Magnolia grandiflora*, evergreen, perhaps the magnolia that is best known even by one who is not involved in ornamental greenery, because it is frequently encountered in city flower-beds or gardens. If it were not so, it would at any rate be easily recognized, particularly because of its large shiny, leathery leaves, often covered with reddish tomentose on its inferior pagina. Of no less interest are the flowers, large in size (up to 30 m in diameter) and a bit

Large evergreen magnolias (*Magnolia grandiflora*).

similar to lotus flowers, with 6-12 obovate and fleshy petals, that open in May-June, and that may continue to bloom for the entire summer. The species originates from the southwest of the United States, from where it was imported to Europe in 1737. It is a tree that is capable of growing to a considerable size, in height (up to 25 m), and in breadth, because of its capacity to maintain the lower branches intact, throughout its entire life. Often these branches act as stolons, becoming rooted in the surrounding land and thus giving life to new trees. The large magnolias are followed by other arboreal species of considerable size, exploited by the breadth and the width of the vast grassy and slightly sloping terrace that precedes them and that makes them more evident. Clearly recognizable, even from a distance, is an American conifer also referred to as a 'Douglas fir'

(*Pseudotsuga menziesii* ssp. *glauca*), a truly magnificent specimen in terms of its conveyance, but unfortunately pollarded because it was hit by lightning. It is a species that originates in North America, from British Columbia to California, as far as Oregon and Nevada, where it forms pure stations or mixed associations with other conifers, on the mountain slopes from 600 to 2900 m in altitude. It may grow to a height of 90 m in its habitat, with the diameter of its trunk close to 4 m. The plant is easily recognized by rubbing its needles, 18-30 mm long, because in so doing it gives off the fragrance of apple. Its cones, too, are very characteristic, because between one scale and another a trifurcate bract emerges, turned upwards, that other conifers do not have. Introduced in England by D. Douglas in 1827, it is perhaps the most important conifer in terms of forestry on our conti-

Rhododendron arboreum in bloom.

symmetry even in the plant kingdom. It is a cornel tree (*Cornus controversa* 'Variegata'), a species originating from the Far East that may grow to 17 m in height, always arranging its branches on a nearly perfect horizontal plane; the leaves, very graceful especially in the 'Variegata' 'cultivar,' with yellow-whitish margins, turn red at the beginning of the autumn, and then remain on the branches for some time.

The tea Plants

At this point the large grassy flowerbed ends, bordered by a small road that goes upwards. We will follow it for a certain distance, to discover other interesting species, but then we will turn back, and one again take the path that will lead us to other areas of the garden. To the right we leave dense thickets of azaleas and also a pair of interesting rhodondendrons, this time not a variety created by man, but a botanical species: particularly beautiful is the *Rhododendron macabeanum*, originally from India, that may assume an arboreal conveyance—up to 15 m in height—with ovate-elliptical leaves that are very large, and rich inflorescences with funnel-shaped or bell-like corollas. Now, however, our attention is attracted to a majestic conifer that, with its foliage, overshadows a wide area, so thickly covered with evergreen shrubs that it is nearly impenetrable. It is a large Cedar of Lebanon (*Cedrus libani*), one of the most interesting conifers, in terms of the conveyance of its foliage, with its branches arranged like 'stages,' and in terms of its history, that has witnessed its close intertwining with that of mankind, particularly in the areas where it originates, in Lebanon, Syria, Turkey. Because of the fragrance of its wood, but also because of its strength and its endurance, it was used in the faraway past for the construction of important religious buildings: the greatest example is the famous Temple of Salomon, the building

nent, because of its rapid growth, and because of its abundant production of wood. To the left of the *Pseudotsuga*, rises another America cypress (*Cupressus arizonica)*, an evergreen conifer up to 25 m high, with reddish bark that flakes and greenish-blue leaves. Its foliage is conical-pyramidal, but ample, so that the plant can be considered a good choice if it is used as an isolated specimen in a garden, keeping in mind that the species grows fast. In the foreground is a truly unusual pine (*Pinus montezumae*), originally from Central America, from which is inspired the same specific denomination, devoted to the famous Aztec emperor of the sixteenth century, Montezuma. A conifer that grows up to 35 m, with conical, columnar foliage, it has bunches of 5 needles, erect or hanging, that may achieve a length of 30 cm, and that represent its best feature, so that it is one of the best pines in the park. To its left, alongside a low Japanese maple (*Acer palmatum* 'Dissectum Atropurpureum') we see a deciduous tree that reveals its very neat conveyance, thus attracting the attention of those who love order and

of which was decided on by Hiram, the king of Tyre, who bought the wood. This species came much before the others—*Cedrus deodara* and *Cedrus atlantica*—in the race to embellish European parks, because it was known in 1638; but it was precisely in the so-called 'English-style' park that it reached the peak of its celebrity, so that, with the beech and the red oak, it may easily be considered the 'pioneer'-plant of this style. Fate—or a precise choice?—has situated under the fronds of the specimen at Villa Carlotta another species that has had an important role in the history of 'useful plants' and of man himself, that is, the tea plant, which is a camellia *(Camellia sinensis)*, quite different from the others that we admired at the back of the villa. A small tree that can grow to 6 m in height, but more frequently a shrub of 1-2 m, this species has rather small hanging flowers, with 7-8 white petals only 2 cm in length, thus, not very spectacular. From an ornamental point of view, thus, the plant entrusts its fame to its leaves, which are up to 12 cm long, elliptical in shape, at times sharp, shiny, and with a dark green superior pagina. They are the most important part of the plant, with which material for the famous beverage is obtained. The Chinese have always used it: in fact, it is mentioned in the *Pent-sao*, a text dating back to 2700 B.C. The word 'tea' derives directly from the Chinese 'tcha,'which then became 'tsjia' in Japanes,e and then was transferred with similar writing and phonetics to Arab, Turkish, and even to some of the Romance languages, as demonstrated by the Portuguese 'cha.' Today, the cultivation of camellias for tea covers vast territories, and this explains why the races obtained have such different names, although substantially referring to three major areas of production: China, India (Assam) and Sri Lanka. Its gathering, which is carried out early in the morning, begins from the third year of life of the plant and is carried out by manually removing the tips of the branches, because the most important part is that of the terminal leaf bud and the more tender underlying leaves.

The tea plant *(Camellia sinensis)*.

Belvedere

Resuming our ascent, we arrive at a belvedere, another typical structure of the nineteenth century garden, that allows us to look onto an incredible expansion of arboreal rhododendrons and azaleas, at the back of which the water of the lake is reflected. A few meters before arriving at the belvedere, to our left we encounter a tree that is a relative of the camellias, so that even its name guards us against possible confusion. It is a *Stewartia pseudocamellia*, a Japanese deciduous tree, that in the Orient may even grow to as much as 20 m in height, with elliptical-lanceolate leaves that in autumn take on a brilliant red color, thereafter tending to become scarlet. Its flowers remind us of those of the more famous camellias: they have 5 white petals that are nearly round with a corolla in the shape of a bowl, enclosing numerous yellow-orange stamens; the trunk is also very beautiful, which is also reddish and with bark that flakes. At the center of the belvedere, shade is provided by a specimen that is currently quite well-known, the *Albizia julibrissin*. Pertaining to the family of the *Leguminoseae*, this plant's leaves are similar to those of acacias, but its greatest virtue resides in its flowers, splendid and brilliant puffs of stamens white-pink in color, that bloom in summer, leaving long, dry and flat pods hanging on its branches in winter. Albizia, spontaneous in the vast Asiatic region that goes from Iran to Japan, was imported to Europe by an Italian naturalist, Filippo Albizzi, in 1745. Other species soberly decorate the site where we are now: a medlar from Japan (*Eriobotrya japonica*), a small, very rustic evergreen tree, with beautiful, long, lanceolate leaves that are wrinkled on the surface, cream-white flowers with a strong fragrance when they bloom in December and January, juicy golden yellow fruits with a sweet taste; a shrub of viburnum (*Viburnum* x *carlcephalum*), a hybrid of 2.5 m in height, with leaves that are slightly shiny and reddish in autumn, and pinkish-white flowers with a very intense fragrance; a young and rare specimen of *Kalmia angustifolia*, an American evergreen heather with small flowers and 5 lobes reunited in a small bowl that is pink-scarlet in color.

If we were to proceed along the path that continues to rise, we could reach the area recently planted with bamboos, but we are advised to trace our steps until we arrive at the large evergreen magnolias and the entrance to the path that descends as far as the *Calocedrus decurrens*. Nearby, a large palm (*Jubae chilensis*, at one time *spectabilis*) is easily recognized for its regal majesty, one of the most beautiful, representing the entire family, originally of the Andes chain of mountains where it can survive at up to 1200 m in altitude. Able to reach 25 m in height, this species has a tall and straight stalk, without branches, rather swollen at the base and particularly towards the middle, covered with scars left from the gradual fall of its leaves, that are reunited in a tuft at the top of the plant, from which they hang with soft elegance for a length that at times achieves 5 m. The fruits are oval or spherical drupe, containing fleshy seeds, seen in Chile at markets with the name 'coquitos,' edible and sweet like coconut seeds, but from which an edible oil may also be extracted.

The Sequoias

Precisely opposite the palm, on the other side of the path, it is easy to single out several young conifers, among which a giant sequoia or Wellington can be seen (*Sequoiadendron giganteum*), placed here to live not too long ago to substitute an old specimen that died a few years ago. The current size of the plant is hardly indicative of what it will be able to achieve, in a few decades, when visitors will be able to admire it in all of its power, if problems of a phytopathological nature have not taken place. At the spontaneous state, it lives alone on the western slopes of the Sierra Nevada (California), amidst other conifers, at an altitude that ranges from 1500 to 2500 m. Easily recognized by its thick and soft reddish bark on conical trunks, the Wellington has scale-like leaves, that are thin and elegant, with ellipsoidal cones that are 5-8 cm long. By chance discovered on the shores of the Sacramento River in 1841, this species was imported to Europe in 1853, satisfying the exasperated search for plant exoticism of many owners of scenic gardens. The celebrity of the species resides in its impressive size and in its proverbial longevity, at least in its natural habitat. In the National Forest of Calavera (California), the sequoias studied have been found to be between 400 and 1,500 years of age, even if the birth of older specimens seems to date back to 3,000-3,500 years ago. As regards its size, in the past, a plant was found, which has since died, that measured 135 m in height, while the most famous specimen that is still living nicknamed 'General Sherman' boasts of a circumference of 25 m, contains 1,700 cubic meters of wood, and weighs 1,500 tons: and to think that all of this was produced by a seed weighing just a few milligrams.

A few steps further ahead, another sequoia can be viewed, but of a different genus: *Sequoia sempervirens*. The specimen that we have before us is young, but if we look towards the left, and up, we can seen the waving foliage of other sequoias of this same genus that are older, with features that remind us that they, too, have something to say in terms of size and age. This species also has a thick and reddish bark, while its leaves are considerably different, because they are not formed by scales but by needles arranged on the small branches in two rows, somewhat resembling those of a yew. Its original habitat is on the North American Pacific Ocean, in this case, too, mostly concentrated in California, where it forms vast forests in the foggy coastal zones. In competition with the previous species, this sequoia is victorious in terms of its height—having exceeded 123 m—but it loses in terms of its age, if it is true that it is 'only' 2,000 years old. Alongside

the young sequoia, is a lovely series of shrub-trees of particular ornamental value: a variegated holly (*Ilex aquifolium* 'Aureomarginata'), an evergreen with thorny leaves and red-scarlet berries; a *Clorodendrum trichotomum*, a splendid Japanese species with very fragrant white flowers, followed by autumn fruits of a lovely metal blue on a red calyx; a winter allspice (*Chimonanthus praecox*), which also has fragrant flowers, that are yellow and hanging, and that bloom in full winter. Finally, again in this group, is a species that was tremendously successful in the nineteenth-century scenic garden, but that never lost its power of attraction, not even during the twentieth century, the *Osmanthus fragrans*, at one time known as *Olea fragrans*. An evergreen, with lanceolate and finely toothed leaves, this Himalayan shrub is popular because of its generous late summer flowering,

Clerodendrum trichotomum with its shiny berries.

the fragrance of which expands for several meters all around. In the garden of Tremezzo other similar species live, such as *O. heterophyllus, O.* x *fortunei, O. yunnanensis*, at times used as isolated plants—such as that which we saw introduce the flower-bed with the winter camellias—or, more often, as components of formal hedges.

At this point our walk is less steep, while to our sides, walls of evergreens lengthen (*Aucuba, Prunus laurocesarus, Euonymus lucidus*, an evergreen euonymus with beatiful lanceolate and shiny leaves), that are a prelude to the large trees. Among these are some of the conifers previously encountered—such as the *Calocedrus decurrens* and the *Cupressus arizonica*—but also a new acquaintance: *Cedrus deodara*, the typical cedar of the Himalayas, that we distinguish from that of Lebanon because its needles are longer; it was introduced in Italy in 1828, where it is still widely used in parks and in city landscaping. Nearby, there is also a large camphor (*Cinnamomum camphora*), of Japanese origin, the true species from which camphor is extracted, while the term 'cinnamomo' usually alludes to the tree from which cinnamon is extracted (*C. zeylanicum*). Even the most careful observers find it difficult to attempt to distinguish the species *C. camphora* from the already known *C. glanduliferum*: in truth, the resemblances are very strong and at any rate both plants are of great ornamental impact. After about twenty meters, in addition to a hedge of *Prunus lusitanica* (an evergreen shrub that is somewhat similar to laurel, but recognizable for the reddish color of the small leaves), stands another conifer, this time of Canadian origin, the *Tsuga canadensis*, with a magnificent dark foliage that we could confuse with that of a common yew, if it did not have shorter needles.

The Greenhouses

At the end of the hill, the path leads to an opening, at the end of which the buildings of the greenhouses can be seen, preceded by several valuable plants: a large specimen of *Prunus laurocesarus*, that on achieving this size proves to be an evergreen plant of considerable effect; a Japanese cherry (*Prunus subhirtella* 'Pendula Rubra'), very lovely with its very thin branches covered with intense pink flowers, that fall in a cascade towards the ground; a *Paulownia tomentosa* tree, from China, that in spring shows off long panicles of large purple-malva flowers, somewhat similar to those of the *Digitalis*.

The greenhouse buildings, recently renovated, host many semi-rustic or delicate tropical plants, some of which are periodically moved to the garden, as previously stated: for a complete list, see the 'List of plants in the greenhouse' at the end of the text. The entire area has always been dedicated to work to support the maintenance of the gardens of Villa Carlotta, but also to a more general technical management of the entire complex, from the times of Sommariva, when the mainly ornamental aspects were combined with the agricultural, sylvan, and pastoral ones. Precisely in order not to lose the historical memory of this important past, a Deposit of antique agricultural tools was opened, using part of the wooden structure of the lemon-houses. In the new building, old utensils and tools used at one time by the staff of the villa can be viewed, also for didactic purposes: a press, a tub, a fire-fighting pump, wine-kegs, wheelbarrows, etc.

Let us now go back a few steps, and taking an excavated path towards the northern circle of walls, we will brush past hosts of hydrangeas and *Deutzia gracilis*, a pleasant Japanese shrub with graceful white flowers; a group of Japanese quinces (*Chaenomeles*) with early red flowers and fragrant autumn 'apples' that cannot be eaten; one of the most fascinating spring shrubs, the *Kolkwitzia amabilis*, originating from China and characterized by abundant tubulate-bell-shaped flowers, dark red on the outside with yel-

low and orange spots on the inside; finally, a specimen of *Weigela florida*, a Korean plant that is covered with long bundles of funnel-shaped flowers. We are at the northern border of the property and, beyond the fence, is a 'Handkerchief tree' (*Davidia involucrata*), a Chinese plant famous for the long bracts that twist around the flowers and that resemble clean hanging handkerchiefs, particularly when they softly fall on the underlying grass. Thus, we arrive at a plateau covered with different arboreal species. We begin with an apple tree with a varietal and nearly unpronounceable name (*Malus pumila* 'Niedzwetwkyana'), the flowers of which are a beautiful purple red color; then, again to the right, a young well-known conifer (*Araucaria araucana*), coming from Chile and Patagonia, but landing with great success in European gardens at the end of the eighteenth century; to the left, a rare specimen of a *Cladastris lutea*, a tree that grows spontaneously in the central southern states of the United States, where it blossoms halfway through the month of June, with panicles that are 40 cm long, made up of white and fragrant flowers.

The Living Fossils

Not much further ahead, a deciduous conifer (*Metasequoia glyptostroboides*), the existence of which, until 1945, was known by scientists only as a fossil remains. During that same year, an expedition of botanists to the province of Hupeh (Central China) found about a hundred living plants, from which they obtained all of the specimens that are now found in parks and gardens. This 'living fossil' is characterized by leaves with linear needles of a bright green color, and by a trunk that can exceed 45 m in

Exibition of agricultural tools.

height, with furrowed bark, that is fibrous and rust-colored. Nearly opposite the *Cladratis,* on the other side of the path, a young *Gingko biloba* seems to want to challenge the *Metasequoia* in terms of phylogenetic seniority. In fact, it, too, has a story that goes way back in time, and while the *Metasequoia* expanded most during the Lower Pliocene epoch, *Gingkos* developed and were diffused particularly during the Jurassic period. The *Ginkgo biloba* is a large tree (up to 40 m in height), dioecious (that is, with sexes on two different plants), characterized by a trunk with a corky bark that is markedly furrowed. Its leaves possess a fan shape, curiously similar to that of ferns of the *Adiantum* genus or maidenhair fern: their very beautiful summer green is transformed during the autumn months, before they fall, into a strongly decorative and spectacular yellow.

The terrace on which we find ourselves hosts other interesting species: in addition to a group of birches (*Betula pendula*), we note a pine with a majestic but elegant conveyance, that comes after the *Metasequoia* on the left side. It is a *Pinus wallichiana,* of Himalayan origin, a species that may reach 50 m in height, with conical or slightly irregular foliage; it is provided with 5 needles per bunch, each of which may be up to 20 cm long, while its cones even grow to 28 cm in length. It was introduced in Europe as an ornamental tree to be planted in parks in 1823, also in virtue of its speed of growth: up to 1 m per year, at least when it is young. To end the list of this unusual area is a North American deciduous magnolia (*Magnolia tripetala*), which is up to 15 m tall, with very expanded foliage and with leaves among the largest of the entire genus, up to 50 cm in length, arranged in the shape of an umbrella; its flowers, which are also large and flat, may even be 30 cm in diameter.

The Bamboo Garden

Once we have crossed the entire plateau towards the west, we reach a stairway in 'Moltrasio' stone, recently made, by means of which we arrive at a second area, until a few years ago the undisputed kingdom of shrubs and trees born by chance. The area was chosen—and subsequently reclaimed—to bring about a 'Bamboo Garden' of a surface area of about 3,000 square meters, clearly inspired by the principles and the techniques of the art of Japanese gardens. The garden is traversed by a path that begins from the stone stairway, and passes under the 'Torii' portal—made of wood taken from the structures of the old lemon-houses—to arrive at a 'room' similar to a *hortus conclusus,* that is divided into two floors: and all of this is bordered by a bamboo curtain (*Phyllostachys sulphurea* var. *viridis, P. aurea, Pleioblastus pumilus*). While the lower floor is covered with a truly dwarf-like species (*Pleioblastus pygmaeus* var. *distichus*), the upper one was planned according to the criteria on which are based the gardens inspired by Zen Buddhist philosophy, in which the concept of a tranquil and serene nature predominates, before which man must only bow down and meditate. In this sense, the main decorative elements of the garden are not of a vegetable nature, because it is instead the stones and the water—in the form of small lakes or brooks with cascades, like at Villa Carlotta—that take on a capital importance: both are seen as symbols of the greatness of nature. The path then proceeds, winding amidst thickets and small woods of other species or varieties of bamboo (the list at the end of the text includes about 25), among which some which are truly rare, such as the *Phyllostachys edulis* f. *heterocycla,* with a stalk characterized by bizarrre swelling and distorsions.

The path with its bridges twice crosses the brook, to descend and reconnect with other areas with thickets of camellias, hydrangeas, and azaleas. Thus, we leave a Japanese microcosm to re-enter the vaster traditional 'English-style' garden, or rather, that which was the first

The Bamboo Garden.

Liquidambar styraciflua in spring, and, on the opposite page, with its autumn colors.

The Heath Family

We instead continue to the right, beyond a large sequoia and an old chestnut (*Castanea sativa*), to reach the fork that will lead us to the 'New wood of the rhododendrons,' that will gradually substitute the old one, visited by us at the lower levels of the garden. To get there we must follow a path, surrounded by high arboreal species of plane-trees and yews that brushes from above the 'Valley of the Ferns'; if we do not abandon the higher path to the right, by going up a few steps we will enter this new complex, which is now at an early stage. The wood is flanked and crossed by a path, that will allow us to also discover the harmonies of two distinct zones of numerous heathers (*Erica, Calluna, Daboecia*), attractive the year round, even if they are not in bloom: an example of this is *Erica cinerea* 'Golden Drop,' whose leaves are copper-red in winter, matching in beauty their summer florescence. Another path going downwards departs from this area, overshadowing the large rock garden, taking us further down, to the level behind the villa. Along the route, if we are not distracted by the panoramic views that now and again appear amidst the thick vegetation, we will admire a large holm oak (*Quercus ilex*), an evergreen oak characterizing the Mediterranean scenery and that, with its ferns, is used in topiary art to shape hedges and green palisades. Much further ahead, at the beginning of a stairway, we must not overlook a beautiful specimen of a *Parrotia persica*, a deciduous tree that is a relative of the *Hamamelis*, that comes from Iran and that, although not achieving 10 m in height, has a truly important expanded conveyance, with beautiful ovate and green leaves that in the autumn take on a splendid bronze color, to then become crimson and yellow before they fall.

Once we have again arrived at the back of the villa, we turn west, alongside the tall hedges of camellias, to surpass the long facility building, at one time used as an outdoor kitchen. A curtain of ever-

to assume the modern features of the botanical garden. The path leads to a large specimen of a *Liquidambar styraciflua,* a plant that is currently frequently found, even in small gardens, because of its extraordinary attraction from a chromatic point of view: in autumn, in fact, the leaves may take on the most varied of colors, from scarlet to flaming red, from purple to intense yellow. The species was imported to Europe as early as 1681, after being discovered in Mexico more than a century earlier. The strange name of the tree derives precisely from 'liquid amber,' because under the bark runs an aromatic and balsamic juice, that is still used today to combat bronchial and catarrhal diseases. From this point we can take different paths towards the villa, for example, to the sides of the 'Valley of the Ferns.'

green shrubs camouflages the building (where the rest rooms are located today), on which two tall Scotch pines (*Pinus sylvestris*) project their shadows—with the typical red orange color of the old branches and the pinkish-brown bark, furrowed with cracks—and a beautiful small-leaved lime (*Tilia cordata*), with its round leaves, or those in the shape of a heart and the yellow and fragrant June inflorescences. More to the west, a small flower-bed has for a short amount of time hosted a particular variety of beech (*Fagus sylvatica* 'Dawick') that has a columnar and fastigiate shape, and that can reach a height of 25 m, with only 3 m in width. To the side, towards the villa, a large circular flower-bed widens, including a mass of commonly-known evergreen shrubs *(Aucuba, Prunus laurocerasus, Camellia, Laurus nobilis)* among which it is not easy to single out one that is much rarer: *Sycopsis sinensis*, also a relative of the Hamamelis, with strictly lanceolate and sharp leaves, that are a bit serrated, and the flowers of which are in thick bunches, blooming at the end of winter. Alongside this plant, a beautiful *Kalmia latifolia* blooms in May-June, a shrub from the United States, whose flowers have a pink corolla and are bowl-shaped, while at the center of the flower-beds two trees wave above the remaining wealth of plants: a *Magnolia grandiflora* and an Asiatic maple (*Acer cappadocicum*), whose finest feature consists in autumn leaves with one of the best possible yellows to be found in a garden, equal to that of the tulip trees. If on the northeastern side of the flower-bed it appears like an impenetrable barrier of branches with persistent leaves, on the southern side, overlooking the terrace that looks onto the lake, it is instead a flower festival, nearly a performance by a very abundant number of herbaceous plants of every type, shape, color, flowering. For a long time now, he gardeners of the villa have alternated the various species, so that for every season it is a high-quality performance. Thus, in spring the biennial

plants will dominate the situation (*Viola, Bellis, Myosotis*), together with spectacular bulbs like tulips and narcissus, while in summer the explosion is even more ostentatious: annuals (*Tagetes, Ageratum, Salvia splendens*), perennials and exotic shrubs of every type (*Cuphea ignea, Lantana camara, Solanum pseudocapsicum, Hypoestes phyllostachya, Strobilanthes, Fuchsia, Acalypha, Pelargonium*). The backdrop of this palette is guaranteed by shrubs and herbaceous plants that are taller, like the *Brugmansia (Datura) arborea, Gunnera manicata, Hibiscus moscheutos, Coffea arabica, Tibouchina urvilleana, Bauhinia acuminata*). Along the wall of the villa vases are situated containing *Hibiscus rosa-sinensis* and the curious sensitive plant (*Mimosa pudica and M. sensitiva*), from Central America, the leaves of which with the least outside

Leaves of the
Parrotia persica.

right, two large and beautiful beeches (*Fagus sylvatica* 'Purpurea' and *F.s.* 'Pendula') rise: the important dark red foliage of the former and the gracefulness of the latter were widely exploited in nineteenth century scenic gardens, even if the 'Purpurea' was discovered in nature as early as 1680, while the birth of the 'Pendula' is much more recent (1836). To compete with beeches is the majesty of some of the enormous plane-trees (*Platanus orientalis*) located who knows for how long right in front, in the flower-bed below, with large trunks slightly arched in the direction of the lake, in search of light. Originally from a distribution area located between Southeastern Europe and Asia Minor, this species may grow to a height of 30 m, with leaves deeply subdivided into 5-7 lobes; its trunk is very beautiful, flaking into large brown pieces, leaving in view spots of pale yellow color, resembling a strange game played by the rays of the sun. The decorative virtues of the plant have been appreciated for some time, if we think that the Ancient Romans used it in their gardens, while its decorative aspect and its longevity were exploited at a later date, for the formation of long formal avenues, along road arteries (as in France and Italy) and in royal properties (the most famous ones in Aranjuez, near Madrid). The cross with the species *P. occidentalis* gave life to *P.* x *acerifolia*, that which is currently used most in our gardens and cities.

The visit to the 'Old Garden' is carried out by walking along three long roads, one after the other, that cut it longitudinally at three different levels. We depart from the highest one, encountering at the beginning a small canal at the borders of which greenhouse plants are located during the hottest months: orchids and *Bromeliaceae* prevail here, but the aforementioned *Calliandra tweedii* and *Monstera deliciosa* are also present, mixed with different species of exotic ferns (*Asplenium nidus-avis, Nephrolepis exaltata* in variety, and so on). This is followed by a stone basin with spring water, that is al-

stimulus close in a pair, abandoning the horizontal position, to then return to it very slowly.

The "Old Garden"

If we now move in a western direction, we enter the so-called 'Old Garden,' the denomination of which has nothing to do with the documented history of Villa Carlotta, referring to an area that, probably neglected for some time, thereafter appeared to be so infested with spontaneous plants that it is, in fact, referred to as an old garden. On the contrary, the entire zone is constantly being renewed, the object of particular attention on the part of planners, agriculturists, gardeners. In fact, once we have crossed a bridge over a brook, we immediately enjoy the vision of large arboreal species and presumably of quite advanced age. To the

so decorated with other plants from the greenhouse, such as the *Clivia miniata.* The path continues in a rectilinear fashion, bordered, above and for its entire length, by a high hedge mixed with evergreens, with a prevalence of *Prunus laurocerasus* and various species of *Osmanthus.* Along the left margin, towards the lake, shrubs and trees of considerable interest follow in a row: *an Osmanthus heterophyllus* 'Variegatus,' followed by a pleasant specimen of a *Michelia figo,* a Chinese evergreen *Magnioliaceae,* that is very ramified, with oblong and dark green leaves, and flowers the petals of which are erect and ivory in color, tinged with yellow and violet margins; their fragrance recalls that of banana candy, so much so that in England it is called the 'banana plant.' Then we find a specimen of a cork-oak (*Quercus suber*), another Mediterranean species the leaves of which recall those of the ilex (*Q. ilex*), even if it is the bark of the tree that is unquestionable, with those corky cracked ribs, that are periodically removed in the specimens cultivated with the purpose of obtaining material for bottle stoppers. A few meters away, a shrub of *Pieris formosa* var: *forrestii,* a Chinese heather is observed, surprising with its cascades of small flowers in the shape of a pot, gathered in panicles but also with bunches of new leaves of a vivacious scarlet red. It is followed by a 'False Lawson cypress' (*Chamaecyparis lawsoniana*), originally from Oregon and California, but today universally used in many gardens and parks, even city ones, in all temperate zones. After a small natural stream, at the margins of which several specimens of *Acer palmatum* in variety are distributed, here is the only specimen of an Italian cypress (*Cupressus sempervirens*) in the garden, even if in the past this species was probably used more frequently, at least at the time of the Clericis. The long shrub and arboreal border ends with a group of hydrangeas and with an unusual and young specimen of loricate pine (*Pinus leucodermis*), originally from

Flower-bed in summer bloom to the sides of the villa.

Greece and the Balkans, but also present in Italy, however rarely, on the Majella and on the Calabrian-Lucanian Appenines. Nearby is an opening, borded by the evergreen *Danae racemosa,* that the Romans called 'lauro alessandrino' and used in topiary art. All around we see camellias (*C. japonica* and *C. reticulata* in variety), while to the right, under the leafage of another red beech, we find three lovely shrubs: the previously seen *Michelia figo* and *Pieris formosa* var. *forestii,* along with a Chinese holly (*Ilex cornuta*), with strange rectangular leaves that are dark green and shiny. Another tree, behind these shrubs, deserves mention: a tall American oak (*Quercus rubra*), spontaneous in the Eastern United States, as well as in Ontario and Quebec, but which arrived here at the end of the seventeenth century, to then be ap-

(We w
Massi
and E
for
tance.

preciated more and more for its red color in autumn. If we proceed to the second level, on the connecting path we encounter another cork-oak (*Quercus suber*) and a massive yew (*Taxus baccata*), in the company of Himalayan spindle trees (*Euonymus lucidus*) and an old specimen of a box-tree (*Buxus sempervirens*). Before beginning our return towards the east, we find a graceful gazebo located on a belvedere, covered with creeping vines (*Lonicera* spp. and *Solanum crispum* 'Glasniven'). From this point on it is possible to once again admire the lake and the underlying 'Fountain of the Dwarfs,' in a cascade with an underlying basin connoted by the presence of stone statues representing bizarre fantastic figures or 'dwarfs,' from which water spurts. Amidst the plants that deco-

Osmanthus heterophyllus 'Variegatus'.

On the previous page: the large plane-trees that lead to the 'Old Garden'.

rate this site, the *Osmunda* ferns must be mentioned, which are particularly elegant, just as we must not overlook the gate that looks onto the road, topped with an arch made of branches of ilex (*Quercus ilex*).

The middle path that we now take is rich with woody species. To the right. an *Auracaria angustifolia*, from Brasil, that in adult age grows to 35 m in height; a palm from the Canary Islands (*Phoenix canariensis*); a pleasant shrub of *Edgeworthia chrysantha*, whose yellow flowers, grouped at the tips of the naked branches, bloom with a delightful fragrance at the end of winter; a rare New Zealand shrub of *Olearia paniculata*, with curious and beautiful green leaves that are wavy at the margins, with small fragrant flowers reunited in pyramid-shaped panicles 5 cm long; a last American *cypress* (*Cupressus arizonica*). On the left side, going back to the path beginning from the gazebo above the 'Fountain of the Dwarfs' we observe a New Zealand conifer (*Podocarpus totara*), that can grow to 30 m in height, with a thick dark brown bark that flakes

in stripes and with needle-like leaves somewhat similar to those of a yew, but furrowed in the middle on the inferior pagina; another palm from Chile (*Jubaea chilensis*); a Japanese pine (*Pinus parviflora* 'Glauca') with bunches of 5 needles, curved and tangled, of a lovely bluish color, and with curious cones in the shape of a small banana; these are followed by an *Araucaria araucana*, a *Cryptomeria japonica* 'Globosa Nana,' that is, a small variety of a conifer, with long needles that curve to follow the line of the branches, that is very popular in Japan, where it is called 'sugi' and is used to decorate avenues and temples. We conclude this review with a *Picea glauca* var. albertiana 'Conica' and a group of *Phormium tenax* 'Variegatum,' a large New Zealand perennial herbaceous plant, which is very decorative because of its sword-shaped leaves, falling on the ground, and that may even be 3 m long. To the right, once we have gone by a subsiding of the ground, where spring water is collected and around which perennial herbaceous plants grow (*Zantedeschia aethiopica, Agapanthusa*

To the left: detail of the bark of the cork-oak (*Quercus suber*).

To the right: *Pieris formosa* var. *forrestii.*

On the previous page: *Michelia figo,* a relative of the magnolia.

africanus, in addition to peonies, narcissus, potentillas, anemones, saxifrages), in the company of a *Cornus florida* 'Rubra'—a shrub from North America with beautiful flowers, in which it is not the modest flowers that count, as much as the colored bracts—we arrive at a stairway that connects the three longitudinal paths. At its sides, a wide undergrowth decorated with hydrangeas of various species and varieties: not only the Japanese *Hydrangea macrophylla*—the most common—but also the United States *H. quercifolia*, with red-bronze leaves in autumn, and the Japanese *H. petiolaris*, a creeping species that can reach 20 m in height. Other enormous trunks of plane-trees shade a group of other species, including an evergreen with very beautiful red and round fruit (*Skimmia japonica*) and *Griselinia littoralis*, a New Zealand shrub, with beautiful ovate and oblong leaves, that are shiny and fleshy. Thereafter, taking the lower level in the direction of the 'Fountain of the Dwarfs' we encounter: a young fir from Caucasus (*Picea orientalis*), attractive for its very short needles and for the brilliant structure of its leaves, which are a vivacious green; a rare specimen of *Myrica cerifera*, a shrub-tree from the United States, an evergreen and relative of the myrtle, whose wrinkled leaves give off an intense aroma. A last look should be devoted to the hedge that beyond a curtain of holm oaks (*Quercus ilex*) runs along the fence towards the street, convincing us that if we wish to create in our private garden a barrier against molesters, the species used here is certainly the best: the Chinese *Poncirus trifoliata*, a closer relative of the lemon and the orange; not only is it strongly decorative because of its flowers—large, white and fragrant—its fruit—spherical and a beautiful lemon yellow color—but also strongly protective, with prickles that are

6 cm long, that are stiff and very sharp. If we instead wish to preserve a more pleasant recollection of the garden of Villa Carlotta, as the historical location certainly deserves, let us look towards the large middle flower-bed and, if it is springtime, let us fill our eyes with the flaming red of the large arboreal rhododendrons (*Rhododendron arboreum*), as inviting and seductive as those on the Himalayan mountains.

Cryptomeria japonica 'Globosa Nana.'

On the previous page: The Fountain of the Dwarves.

Villa Carlotta

The scarce amount of documentation relative to the building of the edifice, probably erected in the place of an old rustic farmhouse, reveals how its original aspect has remained substantially unchanged up to the present. The most revealing testimony is constituted by the five plates illustrated by Marc'Antonio Dal Re who devoted to the Marquis Antonio Giorgio, the great-grandson of Giorgio II Clerici, the second volume of his *Ville di Delizia*, published in 1743. Indicated by the Maria Theresa land registry with different names, 'Clerica,' 'La Clerice,' and 'La Clerici,' the villa, planned by an unknown architect, betrays an architectural style based on traditional canons of the Lombard High Baroque, disregarded only in the central facade, which is slighly moved back in relation to the posterior facade. A peculiar feature of the excellent scenographic complex is the rigorously symmetrical distribution of the different levels, scanned by terraces and stairways that overlap, and that are arranged specularly around a central axis. It is constituted by an entrance from the lake, a gate, a fountain, the stairways of the garden, the main entrance, the parlour, as far as the magnificent back courtyard, decorated with statues and antique vases, where this sequence ended with the colossal statue of Hercules crushing the Hydra, the family emblem, located in the niche of the central aedicula. The entire planimetric positioning of the complex responded, in the intentions of the anonymous architect, to rigorously symmetrical rules, from the twin orators at the extreme ends of the property towards the lake (one of which constitutes the current Sommariva chapel), to the cottages and to the service building, the greenhouses, and the fishponds, as far as the two identical 'Italian-style' gardens located on the last terrace, to which corresponded, according to Dal Re's testimony, two Italian parterres to the sides of the fountain of the dolphin.

The same planimetric arrangement of the ground floor, currently unchanged in relation to the original, seems to respond to the same intentions of rigorous symmetry. The door towards the lake is original, the antechamber, and the elliptical staircase to the left that leads to the private apartments of the two upper floors are identical. Instead, the double flight of stairs to the right no longer exists. The first and the second floors were instead changed by the various owners, by subdividing the area into small rooms, with ceilings lowered by

artifical vaults in plaster. Only recently removed, they hid the current wooden ceilings, where tempera was used to decorate them with eighteenth-century motifs (masks, festoons, and scrolls), the only evidence of the original decorations.

Between 1815 and 1817, Sommariva made some changes that gave the building its current sober aspect. These are revealed in a print dated 1818, engraved by G. Zancon based on the drawing by G.B. Bosio, from a view painted in 1819, ordered by Sommariva himself, by the French J. J. X. Bidauld (the property of the Academy of Brera in Milan, the painting is currently kept at Villa Carlotta), and by a second view, accomplished by Giuseppe Bisi in 1822, currently exhibited alongside the previous one. Sommariva's intervention is due the addition, above the moulding of the facade, of a balustrade with a central clock, that picks up the rustic pilaster strips motif, scanned by seven pinnacles in the shape of stylized vases; the transformation of the window under the clock and of the central ones to the sides into open galleries; the demolition of several surrounding edifices (the two lateral mansards, the small houses at the end of the terraced levels, and the chapel to the right). What perhaps more incisively characterized the redesigning desired by Sommariva were the changes made inside: respectful of the planimetry, they above all involved the original Baroque furnishings, which were completely eliminated. The rooms, described one by one along with the works in the guide published in 1831 by Davide Bertolotti, were thus more sober and perfectly functional to the exhibition of the art collections. It was precisely to be able to more easily admire the splendid collection of sculptures that Sommariva had two lunettes opened on the posterior facade at the level of the mezzanine. The late nineteenth-century neo-Renaissance decorations instead go back to the period when the property belonged to the Sassonia Meinengens; the period was characterized by heavy furnishings in style; the Central Parlour, and the Plaster Room were the only ones to remain in the previous neoclassical style. The decorations of the large gallery on the second floor, adorned with grotesques of neo-Pompeiian taste, and those of the antechamber looking onto the facade with two mythological scenes representing the *Encounter Between Mercury and Venus* and *The Battle Between the Amazons and Bellerophontes*, dated

Villa Sommariva, engraving by G. Lepaulle on a drawing by Emilia Seillière.

the last decade of the nineteenth century, are probably the work of an anonymous dilettante of the Sassonia house.

Finally, Ludovico Pogliaghi (Milan 1857-Varese 1950) is attributed the last decorative work produced during the first decade of the twentieth century in neo-sixteenth-century style, according to the fashion of the moment, that involved most of the rooms on the ground floor.

Villa Carlotta from the main gate.

Villa Carlotta: Visit to the Museum

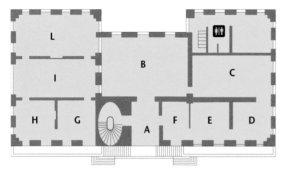

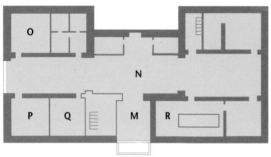

The collection of works of art contained at Villa Carlotta is made up of nuclei of different origins: the first, and most important one, derives from the Sommariva collection, represented only by a part of the very numerous works by which it was composed, in particular, sculptural, which came to us nearly intact, unlike the pictorial one, at the time very rich and also constituted by specimens of ancient art, but the current evidence of which consists only in several nineteenth-century paintings. During the period when the property belonged to the Sassonia Meinengens, numerous works were, in fact, transferred. The Sommariva nucleus also contains a series of furnishings coming from the Palazzo Reale of Milan, that had survived the bombing of 1943, and that were placed here in a deposit; although extraneous to the events of the villa, they are perfectly integrated in the neoclassical route that Sommariva so desired, documenting one of the most significant examples of public collecting. Of equal origin are the series of frescoes dedicated to the Napoleonic apotheosis and painted by Andrea Appiani

for the *Throne Room* of the Palazzo Reale, the only surviving testimony of the artist's intervention in the prestigious Milanese residence. Three statues by Pompeo Marchesi, Camillo Pacetti, and Gaetano Monti come from the Veneranda Fabbrica of the Duomo di Milano. The rare testimonies of Sommariva's nineteenth-century pictorial collection have been integrated with five paintings by Francesco Hayez deposited by the Academy of Brera and exhibited alongside the famous *The Last Adieu of Juliet and Romeo*, a work commissioned in 1823, that was extraordinarily successful. The *View of Villa Sommariva* by J. J. X. Bidauld is also from the Academy of Brera, which was bestowed upon the collection of the Academy by Sommariva himself in 1889 together with six other paintings and two busts of the count's collection, and the *Portrait of Emilio Sommariva* by Eliseo Sala, a work pertaining to the bequest of Emilia Sommariva Seillière of 1873 (made up of portraits, sculptures, her father-in-law's collection of miniatures, and some jewelry) with which she intended to pay homage to the famous family

One of the twelve statues that decorate the balustrade.

main entrance, the large shaped eighteenth-century basin is decorated, in the center, with a statue where a cupid is straddling a dolphin that represents Arion. The main facade, on three levels, is vertically scanned by pilaster strips, two at the corners and the other four central, and horizontally by bands marking the levels.

The Atrium

This room, which is reached through an entrance bordered by two granite columns, was decorated at the beginning of the twentieth century by the bottega of Ludovico Pogliaghi (Milan 1857-Varese 1950) with mythological scenes. Against the lateral walls are two statues in Candoglia marble originating from the spires of the Duomo of Milan where they were removed in 1958 because they were likely to fall: *Santa Domnina Vergine e Martire*, produced in 1812 by Gaetano Monti (Ravenna 1776-Milan 1847) and situated in 1824 on the spire of the third order in the area corresponding to the transept, and a *Santo Martire*, probably dated the beginning of the nineteenth century, and attributed to Camillo Pacetti (Rome 1758-Milan 1826). to this is added a Candoglia marble statue of taken from a spire of the Duomo in Milan until recently located in the back courtyard: produced in 1830 by Pompeo Marchesi (Saltrio 1738-Milan 1858) it represents *San Gorimedone* who holds in his right hand the palm of martyrdom and constitutes a successful example of nineteenth-century purist sculpture.

The Central Parlour or Statue Room

This room, together with the Plaster Room, is the only evidence to the interior decoration ordered by Sommariva. The carinate vault is painted in coffers, stars and rosettes in fake stuccowork, according to neoclassical decorative taste. It may probably be attributed to the bottega of Giocondo Albertolli (Bedano 1742-Milan 1839). Under the vault, along the perimeter of the room, is located one of the most significant works of the Sommariva collection: the

that was by then extinct.

The arrangement of the Sommariva collection, as it appeared at the death of Gian Battista, is reported in the appendix.

The Outside

The garden opposite the main entrance is bordered by a stone balustrade that is slightly concave, decorated with twelve statues of mythological divinities in Candoglia marble, representing, from left to right: Night, Hercules, Deianira, Zephyrus, Flora, Apollo, America, Pomona, Vertumnus, Galatea, Echo, Aurora. They date back to the first years of the eighteenth century, thus to the period when the arrangement of the garden desired by the Clericis was brought about. The wrought iron railings instead goes back to the period when the property belonged to the Sassonias: the 'C' monogram stands for Carlotta, and it is enclosed in an oval topped with a ducal coronet of the Sassonia Meinengens.

At the foot of the staircase that leads to the

View of the Central
Parlour and detail of
the ceiling.

Three slabs of the frieze by Berthel Thorvaldsen: above, Peace turned towards the quadriga guided by winged Victory; on the opposite page, an elephant with the spoils of war and a slave king; self-portrait of the sculptor indicating the finished work to his client.

high relief made up of thirty-three Carrara marble slabs, depicting the *Entrance of Alexander the Great in Babylonia*, a work of art by the Danish sculptor Berthel Thorvaldsen (Copenhagen 1768-1844). Inspired by the *Triumph of Alexander in Babylonia* by Charles Le Brun engraved by Audan, the frieze may evidently be related to the reliefs of the Parthenon, that have recently been transferred to London, and made known throughout Europe by means of a series of copies. The work was brought about in a first version in stucco for the third Emperor's Room at the Quirinale (the current Sala della Marquesa, frescoed by Giani) on the occasion of Napoleon's visit. Completed in June 1812, it was so successful that Napoleon ordered that a replica be made for the Pantheon in Paris. The changed political conditions, however, arrested the very costly purchase (the figure came to 320,000 francs) that was paid in 1818 by Sommariva. The thirty-three slabs that make up the frieze then arrived in several installments in Tremezzo between 1818 and 1828, thus up to two years after Sommariva's death, and they were paid the enormous figure of 400,000 francs, plus 100,000 francs for the marble and transportation. According to several testi-

monies, in 1822 some of the slabs were situated in the *Grande Galleria* on the second floor, while the complete frieze was not exhibited in its current location until 1831. The success of the work, important to the evolution of purist sculpture in Italy, is documented not only by a third version, produced between 1829 and 1831 for the Royal Castle of Christiansborg in Denmark, but also by a rich and diffused series of copies and reproductions. From left to right the following subjects are represented: a fisherman and a boat filled with goods, alongside the allegorical representation of the Euphrates River; the entrance to the city of Babylonia; a Chaldean soothsayer with a crystal globe, a wizard with a baton and a prophet, preceded by the donation of horses, lions, and panthers; the sacred flutists that accompany Bagophanes, the treasurer of Darius; the dancers that scatter flowers and Mazzeo, satrap of Babylonia, with the children; Peace turned towards the quadriga, guided by winged Victory, where Alexander is situated; this is followed by two squires with weapons and two palfreniers that hold back the horse Bucephalus; the general, the cavalry, and the infantry; an elephant with the spoils of war and a slave king; an

Achaean knight and a squire; the next to the last character at the far end of the frieze is a self-portrait of the sculptor, in a short tunic, indicating the finished work to Sommariva.

At the center of the room, on a precious pedestal of vari-colored marble from the quarries of Varenna, is located the monumental group of sixteenth century inspira- tion, in Carrara marble, *Venus Detaining Mars*, a work by Luigi Acquisti (Forlì 1745-Bologna 1823). Made in Rome in 1805, it was commissioned by Sommariva with the explicit intent to celebrate the peace brought about by the Napoleonic regime. This purpose justifies the privileged posi- tion of the work raised on a precious monolithic block in 1822.

Luigi Acquisti, *Venus Detaining Mars.*

Pietro Fontana, *Italic Head of Venus.*

Adamo Tadolini, *Amor and Psyche Reclining.*

Pietro Fontana,
Paris.

Luigi Acquisti,
*Bust of Gian Battista
Sommariva.*

Repentant Magdalene,
anonymous copy
from Canova.

On the wall to the left, in relation to the entrance, we encounter a copy in Carrara marble of the *Italic Head of Venus* (Leningrad, Hermitage Museum) by Antonio Canova (Possagno 1757-Venice 1822), made between 1820 and 1830 by Pietro Fontana (Carrara 1787-1858). As the originals could not be guaranteed, Sommariva often ordered that replicas of works by his beloved Canova be made, and these were often also reproduced in cameo, as in the case of *Paris* or of the *Three Graces*. To this series of copies is added the most popular work of the Sommariva collection, celebrated by illustrious visitors of the villa such as Gustav Flaubert, the group of *Amor and Psyche Reclining* in Carrara marble by Adamo Tadolini (Bologna 1788-Rome 1868), Canova's favorite pupil: in fact, it is a replica of the Canovian group produced for the Russian Prince Yussupoff (today kept in Leningrad, Hermitage Museum) derived, in turn, from the autographed model that the master gave his pupil authorizing its reproduction (purchased in 1905 by Isaac Strauss from the heirs of Tadolini, and today found at the Metropolitan Museum in New York). Tadolini ably exploited Canova's concession by making a numerous series of copies for prestigious clients among which Sommari-

va, that, in 1819, during a visit to the artist's Roman study, on seeing the version prepared for the Prince of Metternich, demanded a copy. The work was made from a block of marble of exceptional beauty, and brought to term in 1824, whereupon it was placed in its current position in 1834 after a probable period of display in Som-

PALAMEDE

Antonio Canova,
Palamede.

Luigi Biènhaimè,
*Amor Provides Two
Doves with Drink.*

mariva's Parisian residence.

This is followed by a bust, in Carrara marble, depicting *Paris*, sculpted by Pietro Fontana in 1830. Inspired by a bust by Canova (today kept in Leningrad, Hermitage Museum), a second version is acknowledged, dated 1831, and made for Francesco d'Este (Modena, Palazzo Ducale). On the marble wall console, pertaining to the original furnishings, two alabaster vases of German production are situated, proba-

bly dated the second half of the nineteenth century and decorated with the effigies of *Aesop* and *Socrates*.

To the right side of the room, beginning from the corner towards the courtyard, we observe a bust in Carrara marble of *Gian Battista Sommariva*, produced in 1804 by Luigi Acquisti and placed on a pedestal that was not original, perhaps taken from the Tempietto dell'Amicizia in the garden, and an anonymous copy, in Carrara marble, of the *Repentant Magdalene* by Canova. The original, one of the most famous works in the Sommariva collection, accomplished in 1794-1796, was purchased in 1808 and placed in the Parisian palace where the count had prepared a specific location: it was a chapel lined in black silk and illuminated by an alabaster lamp. Bestowed in 1839 upon the Marquis Aguado, in 1843 it was handed over to the Duke of Galliera, and today it is preserved in Genoa (Museo di Palazzo Bianco).

At the center of the wall is *Palamede*, Canova's work of art, made of Carrara mar-

ble between 1803 and 1804. The son of Nauplius, king of Euobea, Palamede was the inventor of the alphabet and of the game of dice: the parazonium that he holds in his right hand, in fact, shows the letters of the Greek alphabet, while his left hand holds the dice, which are no longer there. It is another subject commissioned by Sommariva because of its explicit allegorical meaning (the hero in fact falls into disfavor because of Ulysses' slander), related to the collector's personal events, the would-be victim of a plot that wanted him out of political life. On display in Canova's study in Rome, the work fell to the ground after the damage to the support structure caused by the flooding of the Tiber. The incident caused very severe damage. Restored by Canova himself (the signs of his work are still visible on the arm, the hand and the right leg, and on the left thigh), the work was transferred to Tremezzo in 1819 and placed in a special room, the *ex-Palamede Room*, opposite a wing of mirrors that exalted the entire model. Sommariva's love

for this work of art is testified to by his request of Pietro Bettelini for the execution of an engraving based on a drawing by Jean-Baptiste Wicar. On the other hand, Antonio Canova was Sommariva's most beloved artist: there is evidence of the relationship between the two in a thick epistolary and in the numerous series of Canovian works in the Sommariva collection (*Palamede, Magdalene, Terpsichore, Apollino, Ideal Head, Bust of Bossi, Self-portrait* and different models in original plaster). Sommariva always had a ring with Canova's portrait with him, and, in addition to the numerous copies in part still kept at Villa Carlotta, he had a cameo made of all of the works by Canova in his possession. This practice, applied to most of the works in the collection, reproduced in enamel, engravings and cameos, responded to his desire to always have near him a reproduction of his treasures, but it also served his precise advertising purposes, and for this reason he employed a group of artists, from Gigola to Abraham Constantin, Adèle Chavassieu

Camillo Pacetti, busts of male and female fauns.

Thorvaldsen's bottega, fireplace in Carrara marble.

D'Haudebert, Luigi Pichler, Giovanni Beltrami, Giuseppe Girometti, Raffaele Morghen, Pietro Bettelini.

Proceeding to the right we find a group in Carrara marble entitled *Amor Provides Two Doves with Drink*, sculpted by Luigi Biènhaimè (Carrara 1795-1878) around the year 1821, and originally on display in the *Bath Room* where it remained until 1858. Also known with the title *Innocence,* there is proof of a replica for the Winter Palace of St. Petersburg.

On the marble shelf, specular to that of the left wall, are located two busts in Carrara marble, a male and female faun, the work of Camillo Pacetti, a Roman sculptor. Of eighteenth-century taste, although inspired by Hellenistic models, they could be dated the first decade of the nineteenth century.

The neoclassical sofas against the walls, taken from the furnishings of Palazzo Reale in Milan, were deposited here by the Monuments Service.

The Plaster Room

Like the Parlour, this room also maintains its original aspect, desired by Sommariva.

The six ornamental panels in stucco, depicting scenes of cupids and small fauns in neo-Hellenistic style, are the work of Camillo Pacetti, who participated in the work to remodernize the villa carried out around the first decade of the nineteenth century.

To the left of the entrance, on the console, is placed a pendulum clock in Carrara marble with an enamelled dial, depicting *Winged Victory and Minerva*, made in 1814 by Pietro Fontana.

At the center of the main wall is a fireplace, the work of the bottega of Thorvaldsen, produced in Carrara marble towards 1820, and decorated with a marble frieze depicting the *Triumph of Bacchus and Ariadne*.

Above the fireplace is a bas-relief in stucco depicting the *Entrance of Francesco I in Vienna after Peace with Paris in 1815,* the original model by Luigi Acquisti for the marble raised above the minor opening to the right of the Arch of Peace in Milan, accomplished in 1812 as the *Entrance of Napoleon in Milan* and changed in 1816 after the new political situation.

Between the two French windows we find,

still in its original location, the plaster model of the Muse Terpsichore produced by Antonio Canova in 1811. The marble version (Milan, private collection) produced between 1809 and 1812, belonged to Sommariva himself, who kept it in the bedroom of his residence in Paris, and it was one of the collector's most beloved pieces. On the wall to the right are models in stucco of four bas-reliefs sculpted in 1811 for the Arch of Peace in Milan: the *Mars Gradivo* by Camillo Pacetti and *History* and *Poetry* by Luigi Acquisti, alluding to Milanese military glory and to the poetic-literary tradition, and *Minerva* by Pacetti.

Two plaster busts representing Canova's *Self-portrait* and *Giuseppe Bossi*, are situated on two wooden pedestals, taken from two of Canova's original models (the versions in marble, dated 1812 and 1815-1817, are found in Possagno, Tempio Canoviano, and in Milan, Biblioteca Ambrosiana, respectively). Originally situated in the Large Gallery of the second floor, they were to belong to a series of busts of illustrious men that was for the most part sold.

The collection of pendulum clocks exhibited here, nearly entirely coming from the famous foundry of the clock-maker Luigi Manfredini (Bologna 1771-Milan 1840), comes from Palazzo Reale in Milan. On the console to the right of the fireplace is the most precious piece, deriving from the Gallery of Mirror degli Specchi of the Palazzo Reale, where the *Reconciliation Between the Sabines and the Romans* is kept, a scene inspired by the painting of the *Sabines* by David. The pendulum clock of the *Muse Polyhymnia* is instead located on the console on the right wall, originating from the Lantern Room of Palazzo Reale, and that of *Paris* and *Helen* made by the Parisian foundry Le Roy. The pendulum clock of the *Ancient Family*, again by Manfredini, is placed on the fireplace and comes from the Hearing Room. On the console to the left of the fireplace, on a pedestal in black marble from Belgium, is located the last piece, the pendulum clock of *Minerva and Irene*, dated 1850.

The Ex-Palamede Room

The room, that takes its name from Canova's work of art today located in the *Par-*

Antonio Canova,
Muse Terpsichore,
plaster model.

Manfredini bottega,
pendulum clock of
the *Ancient Family*.

Jean-Baptiste Wicar,
A Reading of the VIth Book of the Aeneid.

lour, was decorated with subjects of neo-sixteenth-century inspiration from the bottega of Ludovico Pogliaghi, during the first years of the twentieth century. The furnishings, instead, of German classicist taste, are attributed to the intervention of the Sassonias. The most significant work accomodated here is the large oil painting *A Reading of the VIth Book of the Aeneid* by the French painter, who was naturalized in Italy, Jean-Baptiste Wicar (Lille 1762-Rome 1834). At the center of the scene is Octavia who faints during a reading of the verses that evoke the death of her son Marcellus. Her brother, Augustus, who physically sustains her, indicates to Virgil that he should cease. The other seated figure is Livia, the wife of the emperor. To the right are represented Maecenas, General Agrippa and the physician Musa. Commissioned in 1818, and concluded in 1820, the work reproposed a subject dear to neoclassical culture and, in fact, also dealt with by Ingres and

Camuccini. The presence of Sommariva's portrait, as Maecenas, and of Napoleon as Agrippa, was meant to imply two of the most relevant aspects of the client's extraordinary biographical episodes: on one hand, his ties with the Napoleonic regime, which he never denied, on the other, his commitment to supporting the arts. Located above the fireplace is the oil portrait, painted by Eliseo Sala (Milan 1813-Rancate di Brianza 1879), of *Emilio Sommariva*, the only son of Luigi Sommariva and Emilia Seillière, who died in 1835 at just sixteen months of age. The subject is depicted in an oval, according to the typical infantile funeral iconography of the nineteenth century. The image was not taken from the living model, but from a tiny miniature possessed by his mother (Milan, Musei Civici del Castello Sforzesco). The date when the painting was done is not known, although it was probably during the 1850s when Sala, by then an affirmed portrait artist, be-

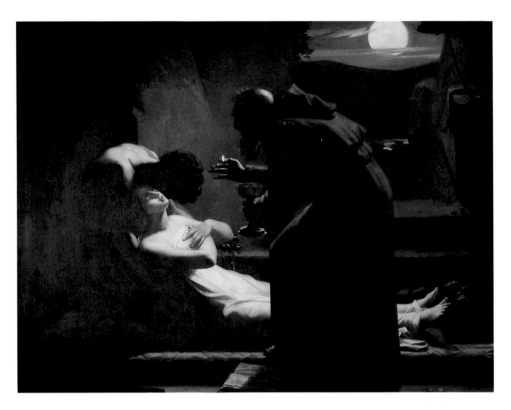

gan to work for the most prestigious Lombard group of clients. The work was done together with its pendant, the *Portrait of Count Emilio Sommariva*, Luigi's brother: both of the paintings belong to the Academy of Brera to which they were given by Emilia Seillière in 1873.

The Hayez Room

The room that follows the ex-Palamede Room takes its name from Francesco Hayez's collection of paintings (Venice 1791-Milan 1882) housed here. In this case, too, the room was redecorated by Pogliaghi's bottega during the period of the Sassonias, the time of its furnishings.

The first painting, starting from the left, is the work of the artist Pierre-Jérome Lordon (Guadalupe 1780-Paris 1838) and portrays *Atala's Last Communion*, a subject taken from the final episode of Chateaubriand's novel, when the dying heroine, aided by her lover Chactas, is communicated to her father Aubry. Done in 1808, and presented to the Parisian Salon of the same year, the work competed with the most famous painting of an analogous subject, *The Burial of Atala*, presented at that same exhibition by Girodet.

The work by Lordon is followed by two paintings by Hayez deposited in Villa Carlotta by the Academy of Brera in 1966. The first is a sketch in oil for the second version of *Pietro Rossi, Nobleman of Parma, Stripped of His Command by the Scaligeri, Noblemen of Verona, As He Is Being Invited to the Castle of Pontremoli, Where He Was a Defensor, To Take Command of the Venetian Army, To Be Faced by His Enemies, is Beseeched with Tears by His Wife and Two Daughters To Refuse the Exploit*. It was a subject dealt with in a first version in 1820, that inaugurated Hayez's success in the Milanese milieu, and replicated in 1850 for the Venetian banker and collector Giuseppe Maria De Reali.

Francesco Hayez, sketch for the painting with the episode of Pietro Rossi leaving his wife and daughters.

Francesco Hayez, *Valenza Gradenigo in the Presence of the Inquisitor His Father.*

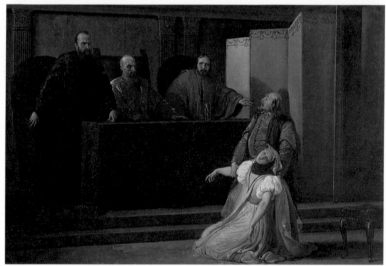

The second work by Hayez constitutes the first edition of *Valenza Gradenigo in the Presence of the Inquisitor His Father*, a subject that, thanks to its strong passion, was extraordinarily successful so that it was replicated in three other versions in 1835, 1836, and 1845. Presented at the Brera exhibition in 1832, the work illustrates the sad episode of the Venetian noblewoman, the lover of Antonio Foscarini, guilty of high treason, judged by her father, who was the inquisitor for the state. Inspired by the French romance *Foscarini ou le patricien de Venise*, the painting constitutes one of the first works of Hayez's successful series devoted to the Venetian historical repertory.

This is followed by the painting by Giovanni Migliara (Alexandria 1785-Milan 1837), commissioned by Sommariva, in

1823, *The Spicery of a Cloister*. It is a typical example of those subjects generally inspired by convent life and brought about by the painter in countless versions. Appreciated for the detailed expression of environment and customs, that conferred 'a Dutch' flavor to the image, they obtained incredible approval for the artist who is recognized to be the leader of this school of painting.

Two other paintings by Hayez, also in the deposit from the year 1966, taken from the Academy of Brera are located on the same wall. The first is inspired by the Venetian historical subject *Vittor Pisani Freed from*

Prison and Taken by the People Before the Signoria. Painted for the Brera exhibition in 1867, it constitutes the second version of a painting done in 1840 for the Austrian Minister of the Interiors, Count Kolowrat, which no longer exists. The work is devoted to the episode of the Admiral Vittore Pisani, unjustly imprisoned for the defeat at Pola in 1379, and reinstated after being freed by the people. A unique emblem of the triumph of popular justice over the abuse of power, this subject, during the Romantic age, was iconographically, literarily and melodramatically very successful, explaining Hayez's choice, probably in-

Giovanni Migliara, *The Spicery of a Cloister.*

Francesco Hayez, *The Revenge of a Rival* or *Venetian Women*, replica.

spired by the *Memoirs of Vettor Pisani, Dedicated to the N.U. Giacomo Nani* and by the *Lives of the Doges* by Marin Sanudo. The second one is a replica, dated 1870, of the famous painting *The Revenge of a Rival* or *Venetian Women* (Milan, private collection), a work inspired by a popular romance by Andrea Maffei. Presented in Brera in 1853, commissioned by Alessandro Negroni Prati, the original version was so successful that it probably convinced Hayez to make a replica in a smaller size. This proves the popularity of the subject, tied to the late-Romantic image of Venice as an ambiguous location, one of seduction and intrigue.

The Last Adieu of Juliet and Romeo is the most significant work in the room. Commissioned by Sommariva, it was presented at the exhibition in Brera in 1823 together

with a painting of smaller size done for the Count of Sconborn-Wiesentheid representing *The Marriage of Juliet and Romeo Blessed by Brother Lorenzo*. Inspired by the famous Shakespearean story, it is one of the first figurative testimonials in Italy of the extraordinary success of this subject during the Romantic Age, constituting a cardinal work of the historical-romance genre. Although the iconographic success

of this theme is linked to Hayez's interpretation, who made four replicas of the painting, between 1815 and 1818 this episode of the two lovers had also been dealt with by Giambattista Gigola in seven illuminated codes on parchment of which one purchased by Sommariva himself. The presence of the painting, characterized by a strong Romantic accent and by a chromatic expression inspired by sixteenth-

Francesco Hayez,
*The Last Adieu of
Juliet and Romeo.*

century Venetian coloration, as part of the Tremezzo collection, of a decidedly neo-classical orientation, increased the celebrity of the work, currently located in its original position, right opposite *Atala's Last Communion* by Lordon, an example of French historical-romance painting.

Finally, a *Virile Portrait* is located here, that may be dated the last decade of the nineteenth century, and attributed to the German artist Franz von Lenbach (Schrobenhausen 1836-Munich 1904), which arrived in Villa Carlotta at the time of the Sassonias.

The Room with Views

Before entering the Atrium we cross the Room with Views where two important paintings are hosted, documenting the aspect of Villa Sommariva. The first, *View of Villa Sommariva and of the Garden from the Lake*, is the work of the French Jean Joseph-Xavier Bidauld (Carpentras 1758-Montmorency 1846). Painted in 1819, it was donated by Emilia Seillière to the Academy of Brera. The second one, *View of Villa Sommariva from the Lake*, was

done in 1822, commissioned by Sommariva from Giuseppe Bisi (Genoa 1787-Milan 1869), an affirmed painter of vedutas, for the *Dining room*.

Sèvres Room

If we return to the *Atrium*, through the door on the left we enter the Sévres room. The room, which takes its name from two extraordinary vase in Sèvres porcelain with a handle in the shape of a dolphin, that has a dark blue enamelled background, decorated in pure gold. It is a precious piece of art of Imperial style, originating from the collections of the Palazzo Reale in Milan, probably brought by the Viceroy Eugenio de Beauharnais. On the opposite wallhangs a medallion with the *Portrait of the Duke George II of Sassonia Meinengen* dated 1911.

The room is decorated with classical motifs dating back to the work of Ludovico Pogliaghi. On the walls are three oil paintings, probably destined to decorative ornamental panels and originating from the collections of the Palazzo Reale, by Giuliano Traballesi (Florence 1727-Milan

1819): *Achilles and Priam, Pentheus Slain by the Bacchantes* and *The Death of Oedipus in Colonus,* painted at the beginning of the nineteenth century. Above the fireplace we may admire a bas-relief medal in Carrara marble with the portrait of *Napoleon During His Italian Campaign,* the work of the sculptor Francesco Lazzarini (Carrara?-1808), that belonged to Sommariva and was originally located in the Bath Room.

The Pogliaghi Room

This room takes its name from the decoration of the ceiling done around 1910 by Ludovico Pogliaghi, who personally did the work here, unlike in some of the other rooms, which were probably decorated by his bottega. It is a complex decorative work, characterized by a reference in Art Nouveau style associated with Pompeiian and neo-sixteenth-century motifs. The liveliness of this sophisticated composition derives not just from the audacious mixing of the colors, but above all from the alternation of the frescoed compartments with the classical medals modelled in stucco: above

Giuseppe Bisi, *View of Villa Sommariva from the Lake.*

Vase in Sèvres porcelain.

Ludovico Pogliaghi,
Ceiling of the
Pogliaghi Room.

Inlaid crib in cherry
wood and mother
of pearl.

a cornice with classical style motifs, four angular candelabras subdivide the ceiling into four ivory-colored vaulting cells, decorated with grotesque motifs, ribbons, festoons, and artificial bas-reliefs with mythological marine motifs. The Japanese-style chandelier was probably designed by Pogliaghi himself, with a rosette in the

shape of a mermaid matched to the two wall sconces to the sides of the mirror.

The Sassonia Meinengen period also includes the curious inlaid crib in cherrywood, gilded bronze, and mother of pearl, of neo-Gothic taste. Above the cradle is situated a copy of the famous *Venus of Urbino* by Titian (Florence, Uffizi Gallery), dating back to the second half of the nineteenth century.

The Ex-Green Marble Table Room or Tapestry Room

The name of the room dates back to the Sommariva period, when the latter had placed here the large Varenna green marble table that is currently in the garden. Three of the seven tapestries, in wool and silk, from the series devoted to the *Stories of Jason*, originating from the Palazzo Reale of Milan are on display. Brought by the Viceroy Eugenio de Beauharnais, they were placed in the apartment of representation, whose ceiling had been frescoed by Martin Knoller with the *Apotheosis of Jason.* It is a seventh edition, woven between 1764 and 1773 by Michel Audran in the 'Manifattura dei Gobelins' and taken from the series of cartoons by Jean-Francois de Troy (Paris 1679-Rome 1752) dating back to the years 1743-1746. They constitute valuable proof of the Gobelins production during the Rococo period characterized by the declination of mythological subjects with sophisticated scenographic set-ups.

On the wall to the left, hang two tapestries relative to the episodes of the *Warriors Born of the Teeth of the Serpent Turn their Weapons on Themselves* and *Creusa Victim of the Revenge of Medea,* dated 1764 and 1770, respectively; in the one on the right, *Jason Tames the Bulls that Guard the Golden Fleece with the Help of the Magical Herbs* dated 1770. The other four pieces in the series, situated on the second floor, are devoted to the following episodes: *Jason Promises Loyalty to Medea Who Will Help Him with Her Magical Powers* (1766); *Jason Conquers the Golden Fleece after Putting the Dragon To Sleep* (1767); *Jason is Unfaithful to Medea and Marries Creusa the Daughter of the King of Corinth* (1773); *Medea, after Stabbing Her Two Children Fathered by Jason, Flees to Corinth in the Direction of Athens* (1769). The neoclassical chest of drawers in inlaid walnut, varnished and gilded, produced around 1776 by Giuseppe Maria Bonzanigo (Asti 1744-Turin 1870) based on the drawing by Piacenza and Rondoni is also originally from Palazzo Reale. It is a precious specimen, originally destined to the *Boudoir Cabinet* of the Duchess of Aosta of the Palazzo Reale in Turin, containing many styles, from that of Louis XVI, to that of Maggiolini with neo-sixteenth-century motifs.

The Appiani Room

From the Parlour, through the second door to the left, we arrive at the Appiani room, so-called because it contains the series of frescoes painted by the artist in 1808, in collaboration with Vincenzo Monti and Luigi Lamberti, for the *Throne Room* of the

Palazzo Reale in Milan. They are the sole evidence of the large decorative cycles done by Appiani for the prestigious Milanese residence, which survived the bombing of 1943.

The most interesting piece is hanging from the ceiling: *The Apotheosis of Napoleon the Emperor,* portrayed on a porphyry throne supported by four winged victories. Located below it is Zeus' eagle, the symbol of the Empire, and above it is the constellation of Libra, the Emperor's zodiacal sign, and the five-pointed star of his destiny. All around it is a chorus of seventeen hours, personifications of cities, regions and kingdoms of the Empire. On the wall to the left are located opposite the throne, *Justice* (with the Napoleonic Code in the right hand, and the sceptre in the left with two

Andrea Appiani, *The Apotheosis of Napoleon.*

Andrea Appiani, *Prudence.*

Andrea Appiani,
Justice.

Andrea Appiani,
Temperance.

Antechamber on the
second floor:
anonymous German
painter, *Encounter
Between Mercury
and Venus.*

cupids, one with a bundle of branches
with a bound axe, the other with a cornu-
copia, symbolizing punishment and re-
ward, respectively), previously above the
throne, and, finally, *Fortitude* (seated on
the back of a lion clutching in her right
hand Hercules' club; with her left arm she
is leaning against Napoleon's column and
holds in her hand the oak crown; two
winged cupids show their strength by
compressing the lion and lifting a shield),
previously to the right of the throne. A

fourth lunette, representing *Temperance,*
seated on a cubic stone while it holds a bit,
is instead located on the right wall and was
originally placed to the left of the throne,
Of similar origin is the very precious, *Table
Mat,* the only one of its kind in Italy, incor-
rectly denominated *of the Viceroy.* The
work was, in fact, commissioned in 1804
by the Vice-President of the Republic of
Italy, Francesco Melzi, to the mosaicist and
goldsmith Giocondo Raffaelli (Rome 1753-
1836) that from Rome had transferred his
activity to Milan. Purchased by Melzi for
80,000 francs, an enormous figure for
those times, it was attributed to the Viceroy
Eugenio de Beauharnais. It was thereafter
disassembled and again placed in the de-
posits. Every trace was lost of the work,
until 1931 when it was recuperated and re-
assembled by Roberto Papini. It is made
up of a base in white Luna marble divided
into three parts decorated with more than
two-hundred loose pieces in semi-precious
stones and precious marble that recon-
struct, in miniature, an Imperial Roman Fo-
rum. At the center is the temple of Zeus,
with the small statue of the god below the
cupola, and, to the sides, Diana and Apollo's quadrigae.

On the fireplace mantle is a bust in alabaster of Napoleon the Emperor, from the
Gallery of Mirrors of Palazzo Reale, and
made in 1805 by the Dutch M. van Lint, active between the eighteenth century and
the beginning of the nineteenth.

The Rooms on the Second Floor
Antechamber and Gallery

From the atrium of the ground floor, and
up the elliptical staircase, we arrive at the
second floor. The rooms here are characterized by the particular structure of the
ceilings that go back to the Clerici period.
Brought back to their original appearance
in 1957 by restoration work that eliminated
the plaster vault coverings, they respond to
a typology known as 'a passa sotto' or 'a
passa fuori': they are supported by the four
walls and a central beam that hold up a series of smaller beams scanned by regular
intervals; the ceiling is supported by this

frame, and it is made up of long axes that are perfectly squared and interconnected. The decoration in tempera on a stucco base, is constituted by a sophisticated intertwining of scenes of cupids, floral motifs, and racemes.

The two walls of the antechamber, ending in a lunette, are framed by stucco pilaster strips and frames. Above a high monochrome socle in pilaster strips, cornices and bays decorated in false high relief, are inserted two mythological scenes representing the *Encounter Between Mercury and Venus* and *The Battle of the Amazons*, painted at the end of nineteenth and the beginning of the twentieth centuries by an anonymous German painter. The other two walls open onto the loggia and onto the gallery decorated with grotesques in neo-Pompeiian style.

The Bedroom

If we cross the gallery, to the right, we arrive at the bedroom, which was reopened to the public afer the restoration work done in 1988-1989. The furniture, which goes back to the Sassonia period, has an oak frame with reddish and veined mahogany with decorative applications in gilded bronze. Against the right wall is a wardrobe with three antae with polished mirrors, scanned by pilaster strips with capitals in gilded bronze representing Egyptian heads. The wardrobe is on four feet resembling lion's paws in gilded bronze.

On the opposite wall are two beds supported by lion's paws in gilded bronze. The lower edge is decorated with a chariot driven by a cupid and surrounded by two flying figures holding a trumpet. To the sides are two night tables with one anta and an upper drawer held up by two pilaster strips with classical heads and a pair of feet in gilded bronze. Between the two windows is located the dressing-table with a green marble top and an oval mirror with leaf and daisy decorations applied. The small columns that support the mirror rest on two reclining sphynxes in gilded bronze. The console dressing-table is similar, with the top supported by caryatids

and a shelf in green marble, as well as a rotating oval mirror held up by small columns that end with pine cones in gilded bronze.

The Parlour

The furniture, of French production, probably dates back to the second half of the

Second floor: the gallery and a ceiling.

Francesco Hayez,
Odalisque Reading.

collections of the Palazzo Reale in Milan, representing a rural scene: woven in wool and silk, it is the work of Francois Var der Borght, active in Brussels between 1727 and 1761.

The Sommariva Oratory

Along the path to the lake, to the left of the main entrance to the villa, we encounter the *Sommariva Oratory,* previously a temple at the time of the Clericis, devoted to San Francesco Saverio. When in 1843 Emilia Sommariva Seillière, Luigi's widow, sold the Tremezzo residence, she reserved the property of the chapel, where the funeral monuments of her father-in-law (1829) and her husband (1843) had been located. In 1855, the building was redesigned by the architect Giacomo Moraglia (Milan 1771-1869) in late-neoclassical style.

nineteenth century, and has an oak frame in reddish and veined mahogany with applications in gilded bronze. It is made up of a sofa with three seats, two armchairs, four chairs, a 'meridienne' sofa and two square benches. The various pieces have legs with the initial part representing the head and the wings and the end part with the legs of a griffon.

The Dining Room

From the parlour we go to the dining room, decorated with a series of pieces of funiture similar to those of the previous rooms, thus, of late nineteenth-century classical taste. In this room is situated the painting by Francesco Hayez, *Odalisque Reading,* from the Academy of Brera: the work can probably be dated 1867, thus, produced during the late phase of the artist's activity, who expresses a subject that is dear to him (the prototype of the Odalisque is recognized in an 1839 version) with that of the female figure reading, which is extremely diffused in late Romantic sculptural and pictorial iconography.

The Meeting Room

The room takes its name from its destination as a meeting-place for the Ente Villa Carlotta. It is furnished with a large tapestry of the Flemish school, taken from the

Topped by a lowered cupola, the building, with a square plant, presents, in front, a pronaos with four Ionic columns, and behind a cubic apse. The small bell tower that is pushed back and the sacristy aligned to the facade on the left flank are also a part of the complex.

The building is characterized by a rich, three-dimensional decoration, ordered by Seillière, that is a perfect example of nineteenth-century purist sculptural production.

Two bas-reliefs by Benedetto Cacciatori (Carrara 1793-1871) decorate the tympanum on the facade of the pronaos and the lateral door of access to the sacristy, respectively: both were done in 1867 and presented at the Brera exhibition that same year, and represent *The Three Marias at the Sepulchre of Christ and the Children.* Cacciatori is also attributed the *Angel with the Holy Water Stoup* and the *Angel with the Sommariva Coat of Arms* placed inside to the sides of the entrance; made in Carrara marble, they are dated 1866. Above the door is an angel holding a medallion, sculpted in Carrara marble and the work of Alessandro Puttinati (Verona 1801-1872); as documented by the writing, it is devoted to Seillière's father, Germano Augusto: "To Germano Augusto Seillière/who died in

Paris in MDCCCIII at XXVIII years/his only daughter/Emilia Seillière the widow of Count Luigi Sommariva/orphan at the age of XX months/deprived of her only son of XVI months/this memory is lain here/we pray for the peace of his soul/and the resignation/of he who hopes/to see them again where death is not."

Four sides of the octagon of the chapel are decorated with niches containing four Carrara marble statues by Gaetano Manfredini (Bologna 1800-Milan 1871) dated 1865, and that represent *Divine Love, Love for One's Neighbor, Religion* and *Justice*.

The *Funeral Monument to Gian Battista Sommariva* the most significant work in the chapel, is located on the right wall. Made of Carrara marble by Pompeo Marchesi between 1827 and 1828, it was presented at the Brera exhibition in 1829, where it was very successful. The central portion of the work is made up of a bas-relief with the representation of *Giovan Battista Sommariva*, who leaves his son Luigi, accompanied to the netherworld by the genie of sleep, wearing a tunic and a crown of poppies (alluding to a serene

death). The protagonist, dressed in a classical tunic, embraces his son, reminding him of *Sculpture*, represented to the right as he picks up his scalpel. A ruler and brushes, represented below to the right instead allude to *Architecture* and *Painting*. At the base, a bas-relief tondo contains the representation of a *Cherub of Death* that, from a cloud blows on a lamp, a symbolic gesture of the alternation between life and death. The festoon of fruit below is instead the work of Giacomo Buzzi Leone (Viggiù 1787-Milan 1858). An engraving on the tombstone recites: "Here lie the mortal remains/of Giovan Battista Conte Sommariva/President of the Government Committee/of the Cisalpina Republic/munificent benefactor of the fine arts/collected the most applauded of works/of the most famous sculptors and artists of his time/he lived LXVI years and died on VI January MDCCCXXVI."

Before him is the *Funeral Monument to Luigi Sommariva* sculpted in Carrara marble by Pietro Tenerani (Torano di Carrara 1798-Rome 1869). Luigi Sommariva is represented at the center of the bas-relief,

The Sommariva Oratory.

Pompeo Marchesi,
Funeral monument
to Gian Battista
Sommariva.

wrapped in a classical toga, and he holds his son Emilio on his knees; to the right, the maternal grandmother Adelaide Seillière and to the left, leaning against the headboard, Luigi's brother Emilio, who died in the Spanish campaign of 1811. The tombstone reveals these words, written by Tenerani himself: "Here lies/Luigi Count Sommariva/intrepid military man/he lived XLVI years and V months and he died on January MDCCCXXXVIII/here also rests Emilio his dearest son/a child taken from the love of his parents and of his grandmother/Adelaide Seillière who so stricken by the pain/did not survive him long and with him is buried her heart/Emilia Seillière Countess Sommariva unconsolable/for the loss of the bride of her son and of her mother lies."

Under the statue of *Religion* a stone in Car-

rara marble enclosed in a cornice designed by the architect Giuseppe Brentano (Milan 1862-1889), the author of the neo-Gothic church of nearby Cadenabbia, indicates the site where Emilia Seillière is buried. The engraving on the tombstone reads: "Here lies/Countess Emilia Seillière the widow of Count Luigi Sommariva/born on XXX July MDCCCI/died on XXVII January MDCCCLXXXVIII/who wanted to be buried in this chapel/erected by her to the dear memory/of her husband and son Emilio/Pray for her soul."

The altar is decorated with an antependium, in Carrara marble, where, in 1854, Benedetto Cacciatori sculpted a *Nativity*. Cacciatori is also the author of the group in Carrara marble that represents *Pity*, dated 1850 and located above the altar. It is one of the most important works by the sculp-

tor, a replica of the group of the same name produced in 1830 commissioned by Maria Cristina di Savoia for the abbatial church of Hautecombe. A third version in marble, originally placed on the sculptor's family tomb at the Cimitero Monumentale in Milan is currently kept at the church of San Sebastiano.

On the left wall of the apse is a bas-relief in Carrara marble, produced around 1860 by Cacciatori, representing *Emilia Sommariva Seillière Crowning an Urn Con-*

taining Her Mother's Heart. A similar version of the work is known, with Seillière placing a crown of flowers on Germano Augusto her father's tomb, dated 1856 and bestowed by Countess Sommariva upon the church of Saint-Etienne in Saint-Mihiel sur la Meuse.

Cacciatori is also the author of the the bas-relief in Carrara marble, walled to the right wall, with the image of the Virgin and dedicated to the wife of Sommariva.

The vault and the apse are decorated with

Pietro Tenerani, Funeral Monument to Luigi Sommariva.

Marble antependium with *Pity* by Benedetto Cacciatori.

Benedetto Cacciatori, Emilia Sommariva Seillière Crowns an Urn Containing Her Mother's Heart.

chiaroscuro frescoes done by Raffaele Casnedi (Runo di Dumanza 1822-Milan 1892) around 1860.

The sliding gate that closes the balustrade in marble opposite the altar is the work of Giovanni Bellezza (Milan 1807-1867), a famous engraver, also the author of the small door of the ciborium with the representation of the *Supper in Emmaus*, of the cross, and of other objects that no longer exist.

The Sacristy, furnished with a precious wardrobe by the Giovanni Galfetti and Sons Company of Como, holds two paintings of the Lombard school, probably dated the second half of the eighteenth century, representing the *Death of San Francesco Saverio*, a saint to whom the chapel was dedicated at the time of the Clerici family. There is also a third painting, located on the wall to the left, that picks up the iconography of a painting by Baciccia preserved at Sant'Andrea al Quirinale.

The antechamber of the Sacristy hosts the two plaster models probably from the Sommariva collection, of *Religion*, or *The New Law*, and of *San Giovanni Evangelista*, produced in 1808 and in 1810, respectively, by Camillo Pacetti for the facade of the Duomo of Milan (the first is located to the left of the main window above

Appendix

WORKS IN THE SOMMARIVA COLLECTION

What follows here is a list of the works in the Sommariva collection as they were arranged at the death of Gian Battista Sommariva.

Large Parlour: where the bas-relief by Thorvaldsen is still found, and to the center the group *Martha and Venus* by Luigi Acquisti;

First Painting Room: two landscapes by Jacob Philipp Hackert, *Portrait of Sommariva* by Robert Lefèvre, *Wisdom Protects Adolescence from the Arrows of Love* by Charles Meynier, *Juliet and Romeo* by Francesco Hayez, *Hunt* by Hackert, a portrait of Francesco Coghetti, a female portrait by Marie-Francois Mayer, *Atala's Communion* by Lordon, *Psyche Instigated by His Sisters Prepares to Slay Amor* by Gioacchino Serangeli;

Second Painting Room: two landscapes by Gian Battista Comeo, two by Augustine Dufresne, one by Achille Etna Michallon, *Boar Hunt* by Abraham Danielsz Hondius, *A Snowfall* by Francesco Fidanza, *View of San Solombano* by Giuseppe Bisi, *Reading of the Aeneid* by Wicar;

Palamede's Room: by Antonio Canova, *Palamede*, a landscape by Hendrick Woogd, two Flemish scenes by Philip Wouverman, ten enamels from the paintings of the gallery;

Flemish room: a landscape by Jean Bruegel, *Domestic Scene* by Peter Cornelis van Slingeland, *The Kiss Refused* by Gerard van der Boch, *The Offer to the God of the Vegetable Gardens* by Gérard Hoet, *Astronome* by Gerard Dou, *Players* by David Teniers, *Bathing of Nymphs* by Cornelis van Poelenburgh, a reproduction of the *Deposition of the Cross* by Rubens, *Head* by van Dyck, another Rubens, *Bathing of Diana* by Daniel Vertangen, *Town with a Scene from Don Quixote* by an anonymous painter, an anonymous *Saint Theresa Who Faints from Mystical Love*, *Saint John* by Gaudenzio Ferrari, *Madonna and Child* by the Italian school, a landscape by Brugel, a small painting of fruit, *Sacred Family* by the Italian school, *Wedding* by Claude Marie Thiénon, *Scene of Skaters on Ice with Skates* by Jan Molenaer, a landscape by Adriano Foys;

Plaster Room: *Andromeda*, a sixteenth-century Italian sculpture, models for the Arch of Sempione, the busts of the Princes of Denmark by Thorvaldsen, the model of *Terpsichore* by Antonio Canova, several marble heads;

Green Marble Table Room: *Portrait of Laura* by Filippo Agricola, a Flemish scene by Nicolas Berchem, *Warrior's Head* by Morone, *Burial in Ashes of Themistocles* by Giuseppe Bossi, an anonymous *Christ Adolescent*, *Portrait of G. B. Sommariva* by Robert Lefèvre, six enamels from six paintings in the gallery, *Celestial Love with Venus* by Serangeli, *Spicery of a Cloister* by Giovanni Migliara;

Bedroom: a female portrait attributed to Leonardo' the *Wrath of Achilles* by Andrea Appiani;

Bath Room: *Amor Provides Two Doves with Drink* by Biènhaimè, an anonymous landscape, *Portrait of Bonaparte at the Temple of the Campaigns of Italy* by Lazzarini, twenty-three drawings from paintings by Leseur and his portrait;

Grand Gallery above: *A Young Man Going to Bed* by Louis Rolland Trinquesse, an antique tablet with the portrait of a female, *Venus Sleeping* by Andrea Celestino, *A Queen Blessing her Daughter* by Mademoiselle Degeorge, *Wounded Love* by Gigola, *Portrait of Ulysses* by Francesco Boldrini, *Portrait of the Young Prince of the Gonzaga House* of the Venetian school, *Portrait of a Martyr* attributed to Parmigianino, *Vulcan that Tempers the Wings* of Love, with Venus and Mars Present, detached fresco by Luini, *Mars Disarmed by the Graces and Achilles Discovered by Ulysses* by Gaspare Landi, *Judgement of Beauty* by Giuseppe Errante, a portrait of G. B. Sommariva, *Narcissus at the Spring* by De Lavallée, *Crucifix* by Lotto, *Psyche and Amor* by Serangeli, the plaster busts of Canova, Bossi, Giuseppe Longhi and other famous men;

Chapel: model of a *Magdalene* by Canova and, after 1829, the *Funeral Monument of Gian Battista Sommariva* by Pompeo Marchesi.

LIST OF GARDEN PLANTS

Botanicals name	Common name	Family	Origin
Abelia x grandiflora (André) Rehd.	Abelia	Caprifoliaceae	Hybrid
Abies alba Mill.	Silver fir	Pinaceae	Europe
Abies concolor (Gordon & Glend.) Lindl. ex Hildebr.	Colorado fir	Pinaceae	U.S.A.
Abies koreana Wils.	Korean fir	Pinaceae	Korea
Acacia baileyana F. Muell.	Mimosa	Leguminosae	Australia
Acacia cultriformis Cunn. ex G. Don.	Mimosa	Leguminosae	Australia
Acacia dealbata Link.	Mimosa	Leguminosae	Tasmania, Australia
Acca sellowiana (O. Berg.) Burrett.		Myrtaceae	South America
Acer cappadocicum Gled.	Cappadocia maple	Aceraceae	Asia Minor, Asia
Acer japonicum Thunb.	Japanese maple	Aceraceae	Japan
Acer palmatum Thunb.	Japanese maple	Aceraceae	cvs. Korea, Japan
Acer pseudoplatanus L.	Sycamore	Aceraceae	Europe, Asia
Ailanthus altissima (Mill.) Swingle	Ailanthus	Simaroubaceae	China
Albizia julibrissin Durazz.	Albizia	Leguminosae	Asia
Aloysia triphylla (L'Hérit.) Britt.	Lemon verbena	Verbenaceae	South America
Araucaria angustifolia (Bertol.) Kuntze	Brazilian araucaria	Araucariaceae	Brasil, Argentina
Araucaria araucana (Molina) K. Koch.	Araucaria	Araucariaceae	Chile, Patagonia
Araucaria cunninghamii D. Don	Araucaria	Araucariaceae	Australia
Arbutus unedo L.	Strawberry tree	Ericaceae	Europe, Asia Minor
Aucuba japonica Thunb.	Aucuba	Cornaceae	China, Japan
Bambusa multiplex (Lour.) Rausch. 'Alphonse Karr'	Bamboo	Gramineae	cv. China
Berberis thunbergii DC. 'Atropurpurea'		Berberidaceae	cv. Japan
Betula pendula Roth.	Birch	Betulaceae	Europe, Asia Minor
Buddleja davidii Franch.		Loganiaceae	China, Japan
Buxus sempervirens L.	Box-tree	Buxaceae	Europe, Asia, North Africa
Buxus sempervirens L. 'Aureopendula'	Box-tree	Buxaceae	cv. (Europe, Asia, North Africa)
Buxus sempervirens L. 'Aureovariegata'	Box-tree	Buxaceae	Europe, Asia, North Africa
Buxus sempervirens L. 'Longifolia'	Box-tree	Buxaceae	cv. (Europe, Asia, North Africa)
Buxus sempervirens L. 'Rotundifolia'	Box-tree	Buxaceae	cv. (Europe, Asia, North Africa)
Callicarpa bodinieri var. *giraldii* (Hesse) Rehd.		Verbenaceae	China
Callistemon coccineus F. Muell.	"Scopettina"	Myrtaceae	Australia
Calluna vulgaris (L.) Hull.	Heather	Ericaceae	Europe
Calluna vulgaris (L.) Hull. 'Ariadne'	Heather	Ericaceae	cv. (Europe)
Calluna vulgaris (L.) Hull. 'Beoley Gold'	Heather	Ericaceae	cv. (Europe)
Calluna vulgaris (L.) Hull. 'Blazeaway'	Heather	Ericaceae	cv. (Europe)

Calluna vulgaris (L.) Hull. 'County Wicklow'	Heather	Ericaceae	cv. (Europe)
Calluna vulgaris (L.) Hull. 'Dainty Bess'	Heather	Ericaceae	cv. (Europe)
Calluna vulgaris (L.) Hull. 'Hammondii'	Heather	Ericaceae	cv. (Europe)
Calluna vulgaris (L.) Hull. 'Islay Mist'	Heather	Ericaceae	cv. (Europe)
Calluna vulgaris (L.) Hull. 'John F. Letts'	Heather	Ericaceae	cv. (Europe)
Calluna vulgaris (L.) Hull. 'Kinlochruel'	Heather	Ericaceae	cv. (Europe)
Calluna vulgaris (L.) Hull. 'Nana Compacta'	Heather	Ericaceae	cv. (Europe)
Calocedrus decurrens (Torr.) Florin	Calocedrus	Cupressaceae	U.S.A.
Calycanthus floridus L. 'Ovatus'	Carolina allspice	Calycanthaceae	cv. (U.S.A.)
Camellia japonica L.	Camellia	Theaceae	Japan, Korea, China
Camellia japonica L. 'Alba Ornatissima'	Camellia	Theaceae	cv. (Japan, Korea, China)
Camellia japonica L. 'Alba Plena'	Camellia	Theaceae	cv. (Japan, Korea, China)
Camellia japonica L. 'Anemoniflora'	Camellia	Theaceae	cv. (Japan, Korea, China)
Camellia japonica L. 'Anemoniflora Rosea'	Camellia	Theaceae	cv. (Japan, Korea, China)
Camellia japonica L. 'Barbara Woodroof'	Camellia	Theaceae	cv. (Japan, Korea, China)
Camellia japonica L. 'Berenice Boddy'	Camellia	Theaceae	cv. (Japan, Korea, China)
Camellia japonica L. 'Bonomiana'	Camellia	Theaceae	cv. (Japan, Korea, China)
Camellia japonica L. 'C. M. Hovey'	Camellia	Theaceae	cv. (Japan, Korea, China)
Camellia japonica L. 'C. M. Wilson'	Camellia	Theaceae	cv. (Japan, Korea, China)
Camellia japonica L. 'California'	Camellia	Theaceae	cv. (Japan, Korea, China)
Camellia japonica L. 'Candidissima'	Camellia	Theaceae	cv. (Japan, Korea, China)
Camellia japonica L. 'Captain Folk'	Camellia	Theaceae	cv. (Japan, Korea, China)
Camellia japonica L. 'Comte de Gomer'	Camellia	Theaceae	cv. (Japan, Korea, China)
Camellia japonica L. 'Conte Cicogna'	Camellia	Theaceae	cv. (Japan, Korea, China)
Camellia japonica L. 'Daikagura'	Camellia	Theaceae	cv. (Japan, Korea, China)
Camellia japonica L. 'Dainty Maiden'	Camellia	Theaceae	cv. (Japan, Korea, China)
Camellia japonica L. 'Daviesii'	Camellia	Theaceae	cv. (Japan, Korea, China)
Camellia japonica L. 'Debutante'	Camellia	Theaceae	cv. (Japan, Korea, China)
Camellia japonica L. 'Dona Herzilia de Frietas Magalhaes'	Camellia	Theaceae	cv. (Japan, Korea, China)
Camellia japonica L. 'Dr. Tinsley'	Camellia	Theaceae	cv. (Japan, Korea, China)
Camellia japonica L. 'Drama Girl'	Camellia	Theaceae	cv. (Japan, Korea, China)
Camellia japonica L. 'Dryade' ('Iride')	Camellia	Theaceae	cv. (Japan, Korea, China)
Camellia japonica L. 'Easter Morn'	Camellia	Theaceae	cv. (Japan, Korea, China)
Camellia japonica L. 'Edith Linton'	Camellia	Theaceae	cv. (Japan, Korea, China)
Camellia japonica L. 'Elegans'	Camellia	Theaceae	cv. (Japan, Korea, China)
Camellia japonica L. 'Fanny'	Camellia	Theaceae	cv. (Japan, Korea, China)
Camellia japonica L. 'Francesco Ferruccio'	Camellia	Theaceae	cv. (Japan, Korea, China)
Camellia japonica L. 'Fred Sander'	Camellia	Theaceae	cv. (Japan, Korea, China)
Camellia japonica L. 'Gigantea' ('Kellingtonia')	Camellia	Theaceae	cv. (Japan, Korea, China)
Camellia japonica L. 'Guilio Nuccio'	Camellia	Theaceae	cv. (Japan, Korea, China)
Camellia japonica L. 'Hagoromo'	Camellia	Theaceae	cv. (Japan, Korea, China)
Camellia japonica L. 'Hawaii'	Camellia	Theaceae	cv. (Japan, Korea, China)
Camellia japonica L. 'Imperator'	Camellia	Theaceae	cv. (Japan, Korea, China)
Camellia japonica L. 'Kick-Off'	Camellia	Theaceae	cv. (Japan, Korea, China)
Camellia japonica L. 'Konronkoku'	Camellia	Theaceae	cv. (Japan, Korea, China)
Camellia japonica L. 'Kramer's Supreme'	Camellia	Theaceae	cv. (Japan, Korea, China)
Camellia japonica L. 'La Pace'	Camellia	Theaceae	cv. (Japan, Korea, China)
Camellia japonica L. 'Laurie Bray'	Camellia	Theaceae	cv. (Japan, Korea, China)
Camellia japonica L. 'Lavinia Maggi'	Camellia	Theaceae	cv. (Japan, Korea, China)
Camellia japonica L. 'Marchesa Margherita Serra'	Camellia	Theaceae	cv. (Japan, Korea, China)
Camellia japonica L. 'Marguerite Gouillon'	Camellia	Theaceae	cv. (Japan, Korea, China)
Camellia japonica L. 'Marian Mitchell'	Camellia	Theaceae	cv. (Japan, Korea, China)
Camellia japonica L. 'Mathotiana'	Camellia	Theaceae	cv. (Japan, Korea, China)
Camellia japonica L. 'Mollie Moore Davis'	Camellia	Theaceae	cv. (Japan, Korea, China)
Camellia japonica L. 'Momoiro-bokuhan'	Camellia	Theaceae	cv. (Japan, Korea, China)
Camellia japonica L. 'Montironi'	Camellia	Theaceae	cv. (Japan, Korea, China)
Camellia japonica L. 'Mrs. D.W. Davis'	Camellia	Theaceae	cv. (Japan, Korea, China)
Camellia japonica L. 'Mrs. E. H. Boyce'	Camellia	Theaceae	cv. (Japan, Korea, China)
Camellia japonica L. 'Mrs. Tingley'	Camellia	Theaceae	cv. (Japan, Korea, China)
Camellia japonica L. 'Nassiniana'	Camellia	Theaceae	cv. (Japan, Korea, China)
Camellia japonica L. 'Ninfa del Tebro'	Camellia	Theaceae	cv. (Japan, Korea, China)
Camellia japonica L. 'Nobilissima'	Camellia	Theaceae	cv. (Japan, Korea, China)
Camellia japonica L. 'Nuccio's Gem'	Camellia	Theaceae	cv. (Japan, Korea, China)
Camellia japonica L. 'Oki-no-nami'	Camellia	Theaceae	cv. (Japan, Korea, China)
Camellia japonica L. 'Owen Henry'	Camellia	Theaceae	cv. (Japan, Korea, China)
Camellia japonica L. 'Professore Giovanni Santarelli'	Camellia	Theaceae	cv. (Japan, Korea, China)
Camellia japonica L. 'R. L. Wheeler'	Camellia	Theaceae	cv. (Japan, Korea, China)
Camellia japonica L. 'Rubescens'	Camellia	Theaceae	cv. (Japan, Korea, China)
Camellia japonica L. 'San Dimas'	Camellia	Theaceae	cv. (Japan, Korea, China)
Camellia japonica L. 'Snowman'	Camellia	Theaceae	cv. (Japan, Korea, China)
Camellia japonica L. 'Spring Sonnet'	Camellia	Theaceae	cv. (Japan, Korea, China)
Camellia japonica L. 'Tiffany'	Camellia	Theaceae	cv. (Japan, Korea, China)
Camellia japonica L. 'Tomorrow'	Camellia	Theaceae	cv. (Japan, Korea, China)
Camellia japonica L. 'Triphosa'	Camellia	Theaceae	cv. (Japan, Korea, China)
Camellia japonica L. 'Variegata'	Camellia	Theaceae	cv. (Japan, Korea, China)
Camellia japonica L. 'Vergine di Colle Beato'	Camellia	Theaceae	cv. (Japan, Korea, China)
Camellia japonica L. 'Ville de Nantes'	Camellia	Theaceae	cv. (Japan, Korea, China)
Camellia japonica L. 'Vittorio Emanuele II'	Camellia	Theaceae	cv. (Japan, Korea, China)
Camellia reticulata Lindl.	Camellia	Theaceae	China

Camellia reticulata Lindl. 'Black Lace'	Camellia	Theaceae	cv. (China)
Camellia sasanqua Thunb.	Camellia	Theaceae	Japan
Camellia sasanqua Thunb. 'Beatrice Emily'	Camellia	Theaceae	Cv. (Japan)
Camellia sasanqua Thunb. 'Hinode-gumo'	Camellia	Theaceae	Cv. (Japan)
Camellia sasanqua Thunb. 'Jean May'	Camellia	Theaceae	Cv. (Japan)
Camellia sasanqua Thunb. 'Plantation Pink'	Camellia	Theaceae	Cv. (Japan)
Camellia sinensis (L.) Kuntze	Tea camellia	Theaceae	China
Camellia x 'Milo Rowell'	Camellia	Theaceae	Hybrid
Camellia x 'Cornish Snow'	Camellia	Theaceae	Hybrid
Camellia x 'Felice Harris'	Camellia	Theaceae	Hybrid
Camellia x hiemalis Nak. 'Kanjirô'	Camellia	Theaceae	cv. Hybrid
Camellia x hiemalis Nak. 'Shishigashira'	Camellia	Theaceae	cv. Hybrid
Camellia x hiemalis Nak. 'Sparkling Burgundy'	Camellia	Theaceae	cv. Hybrid
Camellia x 'Showa-no-hikari'	Camellia	Theaceae	cv. Higo
Camellia x williamsii W.W. Sm. 'Debbie'	Camellia	Theaceae	Hybrid
Camellia x williamsii W.W. Sm. 'Donation'	Camellia	Theaceae	Hybrid
Camellia x williamsii W.W. Sm. 'Elegant Beauty'	Camellia	Theaceae	Hybrid
Camellia x williamsii W.W. Sm. 'Elsie Jury'	Camellia	Theaceae	Hybrid
Camellia x williamsii W.W. Sm. 'Citation'	Camellia	Theaceae	Hybrid
Capparis spinosa L.	Caper tree	Capparidaceae	Europe, Asia, Oceania
Castanea sativa Mill.	Chestnut	Fagaceae	Europe, Africa, Asia
Ceanothus x delilianus Spach. 'Gloire de Versailles'		Rhamnaceae	Hybrid
Cedrus atlantica (Endl.) Carr.	Atlas cedar	Pinaceae	North Africa
Cedrus deodara (D. Don) G. Don.	Deodar cedar	Pinaceae	Himalaya
Cedrus libani A. Rich.	Cedar of Lebanon	Pinaceae	Lebanon, Syria, Turkey
Celtis australis L.	Nettle tree	Ulmaceae	Mediterranean, Middle East
Ceratostigma plumbaginoides Bunge.		Plumbaginaceae	China
Ceratostigma willmottianum Stapf.		Plumbaginaceae	China, Tibet
Cercis siliquastrum L.	Judas tree	Leguminosae	Mediterranean
Cestrum elegans (Brongn.) Schldl.		Solanaceae	Mexico
Chaenomeles japonica (Thunb.) Spach.	Japanese quince	Rosaceae	Japan
Chaenomeles speciosa (Sweet) Nach.	Chinese quince	Rosaceae	China
Chaenomeles x superba (Frahm) Rehd.	Japanese quince	Rosaceae	Hybrid
Chamaecyparis lawsoniana (Murray) Parl.	False Lawson cypress	Cupressaceae	U.S.A.
Chamaecyparis obtusa (Sieb. & Zucc.) Endl. 'Nana Gracilis'	Hinoki cypress	Cupressaceae	cv. (Japan)
Chamaerops humilis L.	Dwarf palm	Palmae	Mediterranean
Chimonanthus praecox (L.) Link.	Allspice	Calycanthaceae	China
Chimonobambusa marmorea (Mitford) Mak.	Bamboo	Gramineae	Japan
Choisya ternata HBK.	Mexican orange	Rutaceae	Mexico
Cinnamomum camphora (L.) Sieb.	Camphor	Lauraceae	Tropical Asia, Far East
Cinnamomum glanduliferum (Wallich) Meissn.		Lauraceae	China
Cistus albidus L.	White rockrose	Cistaceae	Europe
Cistus salvifolius L.	Sage-leaf rockrose	Cistaceae	Europe
Citrus aurantium L.	Sour-orange tree	Rutaceae	Southeastern Asia
Citrus aurantium L. *x reticulata* Blanco		Rutaceae	Hybrid
Citrus aurantium L. *x sinensis* (L.) Osbeck		Rutaceae	Hybrid
Citrus bergamia Risso & Poit.	Bergamot	Rutaceae	Europe
Citrus grandis Oesbeck *x paradisi* Macfad. in Hook.		Rutaceae	Hybrid
Citrus limon (L.) Burm. f.	Lemon	Rutaceae	Asia
Citrus limon (L.) Burm. f. *x medica* L.		Rutaceae	Hybrid
Citrus limon (L.) Burm. f. *x aurantium* L.		Rutaceae	Hybrid
Citrus medica L.	Cedar	Rutaceae	Unknown-cultivated
Citrus medica L. *x aurantium* L.		Rutaceae	Hybrid
Citrus medica L. *x sinensis* (L.) Osbeck		Rutaceae	Hybrid
Citrus myrtifolia Raf.	Myrtle-leaved orange	Rutaceae	Unknown-cultivated
Citrus reticulata Blanco	Mandarin orange	Rutaceae	Southeastern Asia
Citrus sinensis (L.) Osbeck	Sweet orange-tree	Rutaceae	China, Vietnam
Citrus unshiu Marcovitch	Mandarin orange	Rutaceae	Far East
Citrus x paradisi Macfad. in Hook.	Grapefruit tree	Rutaceae	West Indies (<China?)
Cladrastis lutea (Michx. F.) K. Koch		Leguminosae	U.S.A.
Clematis montana Buch.-Ham ex DC.	Clematis	Ranunculaceae	China, Himalaya
Clematis vitalba L.	Clematis	Ranunculaceae	Europe, Asia
Clerodendrum trichotomum Thunb.		Verbenaceae	Japan
Colletia cruciata Gillies & Hook.		Rhamnaceae	Uruguay, Brasil
Cordyline australis (Forst.) Endl.		Agavaceae	New Zealand
Cordyline australis (Forst.) Endl. 'Purpurea'		Agavaceae	cv. (New Zealand)
Cornus controversa Hemsl. 'Variegata'	Cornel tree	Cornaceae	cv. (Japan, China, Himalaya)
Cornus florida L.		Cornaceae	North America
Corylus avellana L.	Hazel	Betulaceae	Europe
Corylus maxima Mill. 'Atropurpurea'		Betulaceae	cv. (Europe, Asia Minor)
Cotinus coggygria Scop. 'Royal Purple'	Fog tree	Anacardiaceae	cv. (Europe, Asia)
Cotoneaster franchetii Bois.	Cotoneaster	Rosaceae	China, Tibet
Cotoneaster henryanus (Schneid.) Rehd. & Wils.	Cotoneaster	Rosaceae	China
Cotoneaster horizontalis Decne.	Cotoneaster	Rosaceae	China
Cryptomeria japonica D. Don.	Japanese cedar	Cupressaceae	Japan, China
Cryptomeria japonica D. Don. 'Globosa Nana'	Japanese cedar	Cupressaceae	cv. (Japan, China)
Cupressus arizonica Green.	Arizona cypress	Cupressaceae	U.S.A., Mexico
Cupressus sempervirens L.	Cypress	Cupressaceae	Mediterranean, Asia Minor
Cycas revoluta Thunb.		Cycadaceae	Japan

Cytisus scoparius (L.) Link. 'Andreanus'	Broom	Leguminosae	cv. (Europe)
Daboecia cantabrica (Huds.) K. Koch. 'Cinderella'		Ericaceae	Europe
Daboecia D. Don. *x* 'Jack Drake' (Scotica)		Ericaceae	cv. (Europe)
Dasylirion acrotrichum (Schiede) Zucc.		Agavaceae	Mexico
Davidia involucrata	Handkerchief tree	Nyssaceae	China
Deutzia gracilis Sieb. & Zucc.		Hydrangeaceae	Japan
Diospyros lotus L.	St. Andrew's tree	Ebenaceae	Asia
Edgeworthia chrysantha Lindl.		Thymelaeaceae	China
Elaeagnus pungens Thunb.	Eleagnus	Elaeagnaceae	Japan
Erica carnea L. 'Foxhollow'	Heather	Ericaceae	cv. (Europe)
Erica carnea L. 'Lohse's Rubin'	Heather	Ericaceae	cv. (Europe)
Erica carnea L. 'Myretoun Ruby'	Heather	Ericaceae	cv. (Europe)
Erica carnea L. 'Ruby Glow'	Heather	Ericaceae	cv. (Europe)
Erica cinerea L. 'Alba Minor'	Heather	Ericaceae	cv. (Europe)
Erica cinerea L. 'C. D. Eason'	Heather	Ericaceae	cv. (Europe)
Erica cinerea L. 'Cairn Valley'	Heather	Ericaceae	cv. (Europe)
Erica cinerea L. 'Cevennes'	Heather	Ericaceae	cv. (Europe)
Erica cinerea L. 'Cindy'	Heather	Ericaceae	cv. (Europe)
Erica cinerea L. 'Dark Violet'	Heather	Ericaceae	cv. (Europe)
Erica cinerea L. 'Fiddler's Gold'	Heather	Ericaceae	cv. (Europe)
Erica cinerea L. 'Golden Drop'	Heather	Ericaceae	cv. (Europe)
Erica cinerea L. 'Joseph Murphy'	Heather	Ericaceae	cv. (Europe)
Erica cinerea L. 'Pink Ice'	Heather	Ericaceae	cv. (Europe)
Erica cinerea L. 'Rock Pool'	Heather	Ericaceae	cv. (Europe)
Erica cinerea L. 'Rosea'	Heather	Ericaceae	cv. (Europe)
Erica cinerea L. 'Sherry'	Heather	Ericaceae	cv. (Europe)
Erica tetralix L. 'Alba Mollis'	Heather	Ericaceae	cv. (Europe)
Erica tetralix L. 'Ardy'	Heather	Ericaceae	cv. (Europe)
Erica tetralix L. 'Con Underwood'	Heather	Ericaceae	cv. (Europe)
Erica tetralix L. Rosea	Heather	Ericaceae	cv. (Europe)
Erica vagans L. 'George Underwood'	Heather	Ericaceae	cv. (Europe)
Erica vagans L. 'Lyonesse'	Heather	Ericaceae	cv. (Europe)
Erica vagans L. 'Mrs. D.F. Maxwell'	Heather	Ericaceae	cv. (Europe)
Erica vagans L. 'Valerie Proudley'	Heather	Ericaceae	cv. (Europe)
Erica x darleyensis Bean. 'Arthur Johnson'	Heather	Ericaceae	cv. Hybrid
Erica x stuartii Linton. 'Irish Lemon'	Heather	Ericaceae	cv. Hybrid
Erica x watsonii Benth. 'Dawn'	Heather	Ericaceae	cv. Hybrid
Eriobotrya japonica (Thunb.) Lindl.	Japanese medlar	Rosaceae	China, Japan,
Erythea edulis H.A. Wendl. & S. Wats.	Guadalupe palm	Palmae	Mexico
Erythrina crista-galli L.	Coral tree	Leguminosae	North America
Eucalyptus globulus Labill.	Eucalyptus	Myrtaceae	Australia, Tasmania
Eucalyptus ovata Labill.	Eucalyptus	Myrtaceae	Australia, Tasmania
Eucalyptus viminalis Labill.	Eucalyptus	Myrtaceae	Australia
Euonymus japonicus Thunb.	Japanese euonymus	Celastraceae	China, Japan, Korea
Euonymus lucidus D. Don.	Euonymus	Celastraceae	Himalaya
Eupatorium ligustrinum DC.		Compositae	Central America
Fagus sylvatica L.	Beech	Fagaceae	Europe
Fagus sylvatica L. f. *purpurea*	Purple beech	Fagaceae	Europe
Fagus sylvatica L. 'Pendula'	Hanging beech	Fagaceae	cv. (Europe)
Fagus sylvatica L. 'Purpurea Tricolor'	Tri-colored purple beech	Fagaceae	cv. (Europe)
Fatsia japonica (Thunb.) Dechne & Planch.	Aralia	Araliaceae	Japan
Ficus pumila L.	Climbing fig	Moraceae	Asia
Forsythia suspensa (Thunb.) Vahl.	Forsythia	Oleaceae	China
Fortunella margarita (Lour.) Swingle	Kumquat	Rutaceae	China
Fortunella margarita (Lour.) Swingle *x Citrus aurantium* L.		Rutaceae	Hybrid
Fraxinus excelsior L.	Ash tree	Oleaceae	Europe
Fremontodendron californicum (Torr.) Cov.		Sterculiaceae	U.S.A.
Fuchsia magellanica Lam. var. *gracilis* (Lindl.) L.H.Bail.	Fuchsia	Onagraceae	South America, Africa, Oceania
Fuchsia magellanica Lam. var. *molinae* Espin.	Fuchsia	Onagraceae	South America
Gardenia jasminoides Ellis	Gardenia	Rubiaceae	China, Japan
Ginkgo biloba L.	Gingko	Ginkgoaceae	China
Griselinia littoralis Raoul.		Cornaceae	New Zealand
Hibanobambusa (x) tranquillans (Koidz) Maruyama & H. Okamura 'Shiroshima'	Bamboo	Gramineae	cv. (Japan)
Hibiscus syriacus L.	Hibiscus	Malvaceae	Middle East
Hydrangea aspera D. Don.	Hydrangea	Hydrangeaceae	Himalaya, China, Indonesia
Hydrangea macrophylla (Thunb.) Ser.	Hydrangea	Hydrangeaceae	Japan
Hydrangea macropylla (Thunb.) Ser. 'Lacecap' cv.	Hydrangea	Hydrangeaceae	cv. (Japan)
Hydrangea paniculata Sieb.	Hydrangea	Hydrangeaceae	China, Japan
Hydrangea petiolaris Sieb. & Zucc.	Climbing hydrangea	Hydrangeaceae	Sakhalin, Korea, Taiwan
Hydrangea quercifolia Bartr.	Hydrangea	Hydrangeaceae	U.S.A.
Hydrangea sargentiana Rehd.	Hydrangea	Hydrangeaceae	China
Hypericum calycinum L.	St.-John's-wort	Guttiferae	Bulgaria, Turkey
Hypericum x moserianum André	St.-John's-wort	Guttiferae	Hybrid
Iberis sempervirens L.		Cruciferae	Europe
Ilex aquifolium L.	Holly	Aquifoliaceae	Europe, Africa, Asia
Ilex aquifolium L. 'Argenteomarginata'	Holly	Aquifoliaceae	cv. (Europe, Africa, Asia)
Ilex aquifolium L. 'Aureomarginata'	Holly	Aquifoliaceae	cv. (Europe, Africa, Asia)
Ilex cornuta Lindl. & Paxt.	Holly	Aquifoliaceae	China, Korea

Jasminum mesnyi Hance	Early jasmine	Oleaceae	China
Jasminum nudiflorum Lindl.	Winter jasmine	Oleaceae	China
Jubaea chilensis (Molina) Baill.	Chilean palm	Palmae	Chile
Kalmia latifolia L.	Mountain laurel	Ericaceae	U.S.A.
Kolkwitzia amabilis Gräbn.		Caprifoliaceae	China
Laburnum anagyroides Medik.	Laburnum	Leguminosae	Europe
Lagerstroemia indica L.	St. Bartholomew's tree	Lythraceae	China, Himalaya, Japan
Lagerstroemia indica L. 'Alba'		Lythraceae	cv. (China, Himalaya, Japan)
Laurus nobilis L.	Laurel	Lauraceae	Mediterranean
Lavandula angustifolia Mill.	Lavender	Labiatae	Mediterranean
Lespedeza thunbergii (DC.) Nak.		Leguminosae	Japan, China
Ligustrum japonicum Thunb. 'Rotundifolium'	Privet	Oleaceae	cv. (Japan, Korea)
Ligustrum lucidum Ait. f.	Privet	Oleaceae	China, Korea, Japan
Liquidambar styraciflua L.	Storax	Hamamelidaceae	U.S.A.
Liriodendron tulipifera L.	Tulip tree	Magnoliaceae	North America
Lonicera nitida Wils.		Caprifoliaceae	China
Loropetalum chinense (R. Br.) Oliv.		Hamamelidaceae	India, China, Japan
Magnolia denudata Desr.	Yulan magnolia	Magnoliaceae	China
Magnolia grandiflora L.	Evergreen magnolia	Magnoliaceae	U.S.A.
Magnolia liliflora Desr.	Magnolia	Magnoliaceae	China
Magnolia tripetala L.	Umbel magnolia	Magnoliaceae	North America
Magnolia x soulangiana Soul.-Bod.	Magnolia	Magnoliaceae	Hybrid
Mahonia aquifolium (Pursh.) Nutt.	Mahonia	Berberidaceae	North America
Mahonia bealei (Fort.) Carr.	Mahonia	Berberidaceae	China
Malus pumila Mill. 'Niedzwetzkyana'	Apple blossom	Rosaceae	cv. (Europe, Asia Minor,)
Metasequoia glyptostroboides Miki ex Hu & Cheng		Cupressaceae	China
Michelia figo (Lour.) Spreng.		Magnoliaceae	China
Myrica cerifera L.		Myricaceae	U.S.A.
Myrtus communis L.	Myrtle	Myrtaceae	Mediterranean
Myrtus communis L. ssp. *tarentina*	Tarantino myrtle	Myrtaceae	Mediterranean
Myrtus luma Molina	Chilean myrtle	Myrtaceae	Chile, Argentina
Nerium oleander L.	Oleander	Apocynaceae	Mediterranean, Asia
Olea europaea L.	Olive	Oleaceae	Mediterranean
Olearia paniculata (Forst. & Forst. f.) Druce.		Compositae	New Zealand
Osmanthus fragrans Lour.		Oleaceae	Himalaya, Japan, China
Osmanthus heterophyllus (G. Don) P. Green.		Oleaceae	Japan, Taiwan
Osmanthus heterophyllus (G. Don) P. Green. 'Variegatus'		Oleaceae	cv. (Japan, Taiwan)
Osmanthus x fortunei Carr.		Oleaceae	Hybrid
Osmanthus yunnanensis (Franch.) P. Green.		Oleaceae	China
Parrotia persica (DC.) C.A. Mey.		Hamamelidaceae	Iran
Parthenocissus tricuspidata (Sieb. & Zucc.) Planch. in DC. 'Veitchii'		Vitaceae	China, Japan
Parthenocissus vitacea Hitchc.	Canadian grapevine	Vitaceae	North America
Passiflora coerulea L.	Passion flower	Passifloraceae	Brasil, Argentina
Paulownia tomentosa (Thunb.) Steud.	Paulownia	Scrophulariaceae	China
Phoenix canariensis hort. ex Chabaud	Canary Island palm	Palmae	Canary Islands
Phoenix sylvestris (L.) Roxb.	Palm	Palmae	India
Photinia serrulata Lindl.	"Fotinaia"	Rosaceae	China
Phyllostachys aurea (Carr.) A. & C. Riv.	Bamboo	Gramineae	China, Japan
Phyllostachys edulis (Carr.) Houz..	Bamboo	Gramineae	China, Japan
Phyllostachys edulis (Carr.) Houz.. 'Bicolor'	Bamboo	Gramineae	cv. (China, Japan)
Phyllostachys edulis (Carr.) Houz.. f. *heterocycla* (Carr.) Muroi.	Bamboo	Gramineae	China
Phyllostachys nigra (Lodd. ex Lindl.) Munro.	Bamboo	Gramineae	China
Phyllostachys nigra (Lodd. ex Lindl.) Munro. 'Boryana'	Bamboo	Gramineae	cv. (China)
Phyllostachys sulphurea (Carr.) A. & C. Riv. var. *viridis* R.A. Young	Bamboo	Gramineae	China
Phyllostachys viridis (R.A. Young) McClure	Bamboo	Gramineae	China
Phyllostachys vivax Mc Clure 'Aureocaulis'	Bamboo	Gramineae	cv. (China)
Picea abies (L.) Karst.	Norway spruce	Pinaceae	Europe
Picea glauca var. *albertiana* (S. Br.) Sarg. 'Conica'		Pinaceae	cv.(Canada)
Picea orientalis (L.) Link.	Nordmann fir	Pinaceae	Caucasus, Turkey
Picea pungens Engelm. f. *glauca* (Reg.) Beissn.		Pinaceae	cv. (U.S.A.)
Pieris formosa (Wallich.) D. Don. var. *forrestii* (Harrow) Airy Shaw.		Ericaceae	China
Pieris japonica (Thunb.) D. Don ex G. Don.		Ericaceae	Japan, China
Pinus leucodermis Ant.	Loricate pine	Pinaceae	Balkans
Pinus montezumae hort. non Lamb.	Montezuma pine	Pinaceae	Central America
Pinus nigra Arn.	Black pine	Pinaceae	Europe
Pinus parviflora Sieb. & Zucc. 'Glauca'	Japanese pine	Pinaceae	cv. (Japan)
Pinus pinea L.	Pine	Pinaceae	Mediterranean
Pinus strobus L.	White pine	Pinaceae	North America
Pinus sylvestris L. 'Viridis Compacta'	Dwarf Scotch pine	Pinaceae	cv. (Europe, Asia)
Pinus sylvestris L.	Scotch pine	Pinaceae	Europe, Asia
Pinus wallichiana A.B. Jackson	Himalayan pine	Pinaceae	Himalaya
Pittosporum tobira Ait.	"Pittosporo"	Pittosporaceae	China, Japan
Platanus orientalis L.	Plane-tree	Platanaceae	Europe, Asia Minor
Platanus x acerifolia (Ait.) Willd.	Plane-tree	Platanaceae	Hybrid
Pleioblastus auricomus (Mitford) D. McClintock	Bamboo	Gramineae	Japan

Pleioblastus fortunei (Van Houtte) Nak.	Bamboo	Gramineae	Japan
Pleioblastus humilis (Mitford) Nak. var. *pumilus* (Mitford) D. McClintock	Bamboo	Gramineae	Japan
Pleioblastus pygmaeus (Miq.) Nak. var. *distichus* (Mitford) Nak.	Bamboo	Gramineae	Japan
Plumbago auriculata Lam.		Plumbaginaceae	South Africa
Podocarpus macrophyllus (Thunb.) D. Don.		Podocarpaceae	China, Japan
Podocarpus totara G. Benn. ex D. Don.		Podocarpaceae	New Zealand
Poncirus trifoliata (L.) Raf.		Rutaceae	China
Populus nigra L.	Black poplar	Salicaceae	Europe, South Africa, Siberia
Potentilla fruticosa L.	Potentilla	Rosaceae	Northern Hemisphere
Prunus avium L.	Cherry	Rosaceae	Europe, Asia Minor, Caucasus
Prunus laurocerasus L.	Cherry laurel	Rosaceae	Europe, Asia Minor
Prunus lusitanica L.	Portuguese cherry laurel	Rosaceae	Iberian peninsula
Prunus speciosa (Koidz.) Ingram.	Cherry	Rosaceae	Japan
Prunus subhirtella Miq. 'Pendula Rubra'	Hanging cherry	Rosaceae	cv. Japan
Prunus x 'Kanzan'	Japanese cherry	Rosaceae	cv. China, Japan
Pseudosasa japonica (Sieb. & Zucc. ex Steud.) Mak. ex Nak.		Gramineae	Japan, Korea
Pseudosasa japonica (Sieb. & Zucc. ex Steud.) Mak. ex Nak. f. *tsutsumiana*	Bamboo	Gramineae	Japan
Pseudotsuga menziesii (Mirb.) Franco ssp. *glauca*	Douglas fir	Pinaceae	U.S.A.
Punica granatum L.	Pomegranate	Punicaceae	Mediterranean
Pyracantha angustifolia (Franch.) Schneid.	"Piracanta"	Rosaceae	China
Pyracantha coccinea Roem.	"Piracanta"	Rosaceae	Italy, Asia Minor
Qiongzhuea tumidinoda Hsueh & Yi.	Bamboo	Gramineae	China
Quercus ilex L.	Holm oak	Fagaceae	Mediterranean
Quercus robur L.	English oak	Fagaceae	Europe
Quercus rubra L.	Red oak	Fagaceae	North America
Quercus suber L.	Cork-oak	Fagaceae	Mediterranean , North Africa
Rhapis flabelliformis (Thunb.) Henry	Palm	Palmae	China, Japan
Rhododendron arboreum Sm.	Arboreal rhododendron	Ericaceae	Himalaya, China, India, Sri Lanka
Rhododendron L. subgenus *Rhododendron* L., subgenus *Hymenanthes* (Bl.) K. Koch, subgenus *Azalea* (L.) Planch.	Rhododendron azalea	Ericaceae	Species, Hybrid and Cultivar
Rhus x pulvinata Greene		Anacardiaceae	Hybrid
Robinia pseudoacacia L.	Locust tree	Leguminosae	U.S.A.
Rosa L. x 'Aimée Vibert'	Rose	Rosaceae	Hybrid
Rosa L. x 'Albéric Barbier'	Rose	Rosaceae	Hybrid
Rosa L. x 'American Pillar'	Rose	Rosaceae	Hybrid
Rosa L. x 'Bettina'	Rose	Rosaceae	Hybrid
Rosa L. x 'Blaze'	Rose	Rosaceae	Hybrid
Rosa L. x 'Blazier'	Rose	Rosaceae	Hybrid
Rosa L. x 'Clair Matin'	Rose	Rosaceae	Hybrid
Rosa L. x 'Crimson Showers'	Rose	Rosaceae	Hybrid
Rosa L. x 'Danse des Sylphes'	Rose	Rosaceae	Hybrid
Rosa L. x 'Danse du Feu'	Rose	Rosaceae	Hybrid
Rosa L. x 'Dorothy Perkins'	Rose	Rosaceae	Hybrid
Rosa L. x 'Dortmund'	Rose	Rosaceae	Hybrid
Rosa L. x 'Eden Rose'	Rose	Rosaceae	Hybrid
Rosa L. x 'Frau Karl Druschki'	Rose	Rosaceae	Hybrid
Rosa L. x 'Goldilocks'	Rose	Rosaceae	Hybrid
Rosa L. x 'Herbert Stevens'	Rose	Rosaceae	Hybrid
Rosa L. x 'Iskra'	Rose	Rosaceae	Hybrid
Rosa L. x 'Kalinka'	Rose	Rosaceae	Hybrid
Rosa L. x 'Korona'	Rose	Rosaceae	Hybrid
Rosa L. x 'Maria Callas'	Rose	Rosaceae	Hybrid
Rosa L. x 'Mermaid'	Rose	Rosaceae	Hybrid
Rosa L. x 'New Dawn'	Rose	Rosaceae	Hybrid
Rosa L. x 'Papa Meilland'	Rose	Rosaceae	Hybrid
Rosa L. x 'Peace'	Rose	Rosaceae	Hybrid
Rosa L. x 'Penelope'	Rose	Rosaceae	Hybrid
Rosa L. x 'Perfecta'	Rose	Rosaceae	Hybrid
Rosa L. x 'Pink Garnet'	Rose	Rosaceae	Hybrid
Rosa L. x 'Porthos'	Rose	Rosaceae	Hybrid
Rosa L. x 'President H. Hoover'	Rose	Rosaceae	Hybrid
Rosa L. x 'Princess Margaret of England'	Rose	Rosaceae	Hybrid
Rosa L. x 'Rapture'	Rose	Rosaceae	Hybrid
Rosa L. x 'Scarlet Fire'	Rose	Rosaceae	Hybrid
Rosa L. x 'Serenissima'	Rose	Rosaceae	Hybrid
Rosa L. x 'Soraya'	Rose	Rosaceae	Hybrid
Rosa L. x 'Speck's Yellow'	Rose	Rosaceae	Hybrid
Rosa L. x 'Vogue'	Rose	Rosaceae	Hybrid
Rosa L. x 'Yesterday'	Rose	Rosaceae	Hybrid
Rosa L. x 'Zambra'	Rose	Rosaceae	Hybrid
Ruscus aculeatus L.	Butcher's-broom	Liliaceae	Europe
Ruscus hypoglossum L.	Alexandrine laurel	Liliaceae	Europe
Sabal palmetto (Walter) Lodd. ex Schult. & Schult. f.	Small palm	Palmae	U.S.A.
Sarcococca saligna (D. Don) Muell.		Buxaceae	Himalaya
Sasa kurilensis (Rupr.) Mak. & Shib.	Bamboo	Gramineae	Japan, Korea
Sasa tessellata (Munro) Mak.	Bamboo	Gramineae	China, Japan

Sasa veitchii (Carr.) Rehd.	Bamboo	Gramineae	Japan
Semiarundinaria fastuosa (Marliac ex Mitford) Mak. ex Nak.	Bamboo	Gramineae	Japan
Sequoia sempervirens (D. Don) Endl.	Sequoia	Cupressaceae	U.S.A.
Sequoiadendron giganteum (Lindl) Buchholz	Wellingtonia	Cupressaceae	U.S.A.
Shibataea kumasasa (Zoll. ex Steud.) Mak. ex Nak.	Bamboo	Gramineae	China, Japan
Sinobambusa tootsik (Sieb. ex Mak.) Mak. f. albostriata Muroi.	Bamboo	Gramineae	China
Skimmia japonica Thunb.		Rutaceae	Japan, China
Solanum crispum Ruiz & Pav. 'Glasnevin'		Solanaceae	cv. (Chile)
Solanum jasminoides Paxt.		Solanaceae	Brasil
Spiraea cantoniensis Lour.	Spiraea	Rosaceae	China, Japan
Spiraea douglasii Hook.	Spiraea	Rosaceae	North America
Spiraea japonica L. f. 'Bumalda'	Spiraea	Rosaceae	cv. (Japan, China)
Stauntonia hexaphylla Decne.		Lardizabalaceae	Korea, Japan
Stewartia pseudocamellia Maxim.		Theaceae	Japan
Sycopsis sinensis Oliv.		Hamamelidaceae	China
Tamarix gallica L.	Tamarisk	Tamaricaceae	Mediterranean
Taxus baccata L.	Yew	Taxaceae	Europe, North America, Asia Minor
Taxus baccata L. 'Cavendishii'	Dwarf yew	Taxaceae	cv (Europe)
Taxus baccata L. 'Fastigiata' *"fastigiata"*	Fastigiate yew	Taxaceae	cv (Europe)
Tetragonocalmus quadrangularis	Bamboo	Gramineae	Far East
Thuja occidentalis L.	Thuja	Cupressaceae	North America
Thuja plicata D. Don	Thuja	Cupressaceae	North America
Thujopsis dolabrata (L. f.) Sieb. & Zucc. 'Variegata'		Cupressaceae	Japan
Tilia cordata Mill.	Wild linden	Tiliaceae	Europe
Tilia platyphyllos Scop.	Domestic linden	Tiliaceae	Europe, Asia
Trachelospermum jasminoides (Lindl.) Lem.	False jasmine	Apocynaceae	China
Trachycarpus fortunei H.A. Wendl.	Palm	Palmae	China
Tsuga canadensis (L.) Carr.	Canadian fir	Pinaceae	North America
Ulmus glabra		Ulmaceae	Europe
Viburnum buddleifolium C.H. Wright	Viburnum	Caprifoliaceae	China
Viburnum carlesii Hemsl.	Viburnum	Caprifoliaceae	Korea, Japan
Viburnum tinus L.	Laurel	Caprifoliaceae	Mediterranean, North Africa
Viburnum x carlcephalum Burkwood & Skipwith	Viburnum	Caprifoliaceae	Hybrid
Vitex agnus-castus L.	Chaste tree	Verbenaceae	Europe
Washingtonia filifera (Lindl. ex André) H.A. Wendl.	Palm	Palmae	U.S.A.
Weigela florida (Bunge) A. DC.	Weigelia	Caprifoliaceae	Korea, China, Japan x 2 volte
Weigela florida (Bunge) A. DC. 'Variegata'	Weigelia	Caprifoliaceae	China
Wisteria sinensis (Sims.) Sweet.	Wisteria	Leguminosae	Central America
Yucca elephantipes Reg.		Liliaceae	U.S.A.
Yucca flaccida Haw.		Liliaceae	U.S.A.
Yucca gloriosa L.		Liliaceae	U.S.A.
Yucca recurvifolia Salisb.		Liliaceae	cv. (U.S.A.)
Yucca recurvifolia Salisb. 'Variegata'		Liliaceae	South Africa
Zantedeschia aethiopica (L.) Spreng.	Water arum	Araceae	

LIST OF GREENHOUSE PLANTS

Notanical name	Vulgar name	Family	Origin
Acalypha wilkesiana Muell. Arg. 'Obovata'		Euphorbiaceae	cv. (Oceania)
Aechmea fasciata (Lindl.) Bak.		Bromeliaceae	Brasil
Aeonium arboreum (L.) Webb & Berth.		Crassulaceae	Tenerife
Aerangis thomsonii (Rolfe) Schltr.		Orchidaceae	Africa
Aeschynanthus speciosus Hook.		Gesneriaceae	Malaysia
Agave americana L.		Agavaceae	Mexico
Agave attenuata Salm-Dyck		Agavaceae	Mexico
Agave celsii Hook.		Agavaceae	Mexico
Agave ferdinandi-regis A. Berger		Agavaceae	Mexico
Agave filifera Salm-Dyck		Agavaceae	Mexico
Agave univittata Haw.		Agavaceae	Mexico
Aloe arborescens Mill.		Liliaceae	Southern Africa
Aloe aristata Haw.		Liliaceae	South Africa
Aloe ciliaris Haw.		Liliaceae	South Africa
Aloe davyana Schönl.		Liliaceae	South Africa
Aloe saponaria (Ait. f.) Haw.		Liliaceae	Southern Africa
Aloe saponaria (Ait. f.) Haw. *x striata* Haw.		Liliaceae	Hybrid
Alsophila australis R. Br.	Tree fern	Cyatheaceae	Australia
Alsophila cooperi F. Muell.		Cyatheaceae	Australia
Ananas bracteatus (Lindl.) Schult. f. 'Striatus'		Bromeliaceae	cv. Brasil
Anthurium andraeanum André	Anthurium	Araceae	Colombia, Ecuador
Anthurium cordatum K. Koch & Sello		Araceae	Mexico
Anthurium crystallinum Lindl. & André		Araceae	Central and South America
Anthurium scherzerianum Schott.	Anthurium	Araceae	Costa Rica
Araucaria heterophylla (Salisb.) Franco		Araucariaceae	Norfolk Islands

Asparagus densiflorus (Kunth) Jessop 'Sprengeri'		Liliaceae	cv. (South Africa)
Asparagus densiflorus 'Myersii'		Liliaceae	cv. (South Africa)
Asparagus plumosus Bak.		Liliaceae	Southeastern Africa
Asplenium nidus L.	Fern	Aspleniaceae	Tropics
Astrophytum myriostigma Lem.		Cactaceae	Mexico
Bauhinia acuminata L.	Orchid tree	Leguminosae	Southeastern Asia
Begonia masoniana Irmsch. 'Iron Cross'		Begoniaceae	New Guinea
Begonia rex Putzeys		Begoniaceae	Assam
Begonia x erythrophylla J. Neumann		Begoniaceae	Hybrid
Beloperone guttata Brandg.		Acanthaceae	Mexico
Bougainvillea glabra Choisy in DC.		Nyctaginaceae	Brasil
Bougainvillea glabra Choisy in DC. 'Sanderiana'		Nyctaginaceae	cv. (Brasil)
Brugmansia arborea (L.) Lagerh.		Solanaceae	Andes
Brunfelsia calycina Benth.		Solanaceae	Brasil
Calliandra tweedii Benth.		Leguminosae	Brasil
Capparis spinosa L. var. *inermis*		Capparidaceae	Mediterranean, Asia
Cereus caesius Salm-Dyck ex Pfeiff.		Cactaceae	(Name ambig.)
Cereus uruguayanus Kiesling		Cactaceae	Brasil, Argentina
Cereus uruguayanus Kiesling 'Monstruosus'		Cactaceae	cv. Brasil, Argentina
Ceropegia woodii Schltr.		Asclepiadaceae	Central Southern Africa
Chamaedorea elegans Mart.		Palmae	Central America
Chlorophytum capense (L.) Voss.		Liliaceae	South Africa
Clivia miniata Reg.		Amaryllidaceae	South Africa
Clivia nobilis Lindl.		Amaryllidaceae	South Africa
Codiaeum variegatum (L.) Bl.	Croton	Euphorbiaceae	India, Sri Lanka
Coelogyne cristata Lindl.		Orchidaceae	India
Coffea arabica L.		Rubiaceae	Ethiopia, Sudan
Crassula x 'Tricolor Jade'		Crassulaceae	Hybrid
Cryptocereus anthonyanus Alexander	Fish-bone	Cactaceae	Mexico
Ctenanthe kummerana (E. Morr.) Eichl.		Marantaceae	Brasil
Cuphea ignea A. DC.		Lythraceae	Mexico, Jamaica
Curculigo capitulata (Lour.) Kuntze		Hypoxidaceae	Asia, Australia
Cyperus alternifolius L.		Cyperaceae	Madagascar
Cyperus albostriatus Schräd.		Cyperaceae	South Africa
Cyperus papyrus L.	Egyptian papyrus	Cyperaceae	Africa
Cypripedium insigne Wallich.		Orchidaceae	India
Cyrtomium falcatum (L. f.) Presl. 'Rochefordianum'		Dryopteridaceae	cv. (China, Malaysia, India, Africa)
Dicksonia antarctica Labill.	Tree fern	Dicksoniaceae	Australia, Tasmania
Dracaena deremensis Engl.		Agavaceae	Tropical Africa
Dracaena sanderiana hort. Sander ex Mast.		Agavaceae	Cameroon
Dyckia brevifolia Bak.		Bromeliaceae	Brasil
Echeveria agavoides Lem.		Crassulaceae	Mexico
Echeveria ciliata Moran.		Crassulaceae	Mexico
Echeveria pulvinata Rose x *harmsii* J.F. Macbr. (*E.* x 'Pulv-Oliver')		Crassulaceae	Hybrid
Echinocactus grusonii Hildm.		Cactaceae	Mexico
Eichhornia crassipes (Mart.) Solms-Laub.		Pontederiaceae	South America
Encephalartos hildebrandtii A. Br. & Bouché		Zamiaceae	Tropical Africa
Encephalartos horridus (Jacq.) Lehm.		Zamiaceae	South Africa
Epiphyllum ackermannii Haw.		Cactaceae	Mexico
Epiphyllum truncatum Haw.		Cactaceae	Brasil
Eupatorium ianthinum (Hook.) Hemsl.		Compositae	Mexico
Euphorbia canariensis L.		Euphorbiaceae	Canary Islands
Euphorbia candelabrum Kotschy		Euphorbiaceae	Africa
Euphorbia grandidens Haw.		Euphorbiaceae	South Africa
Euphorbia ingens E. Mey.		Euphorbiaceae	Central Southern Africa
Euphorbia ingens E. Mey. 'Triangularis'		Euphorbiaceae	cv. (Central Southern Africa)
Euphorbia obesa Hook. f.		Euphorbiaceae	South Africa
Euphorbia pulcherrima Willd. ex Klotzsch.	Poinsettia	Euphorbiaceae	Mexico
Euphorbia pseudocactus A. Berger.		Euphorbiaceae	South Africa
Euphorbia ramipressa Croizat		Euphorbiaceae	Cultivated
Euphorbia splendens Bojer ex Hook.		Euphorbiaceae	Madagascar
Euphorbia triangularis Desf.		Euphorbiaceae	South Africa
Ferocactus pringlei (J. Coult.) Britt. & Rose		Cactaceae	Mexico
Ficus benjamina L. 'Starlight'		Moraceae	Asia, Australia, Pacific
Ficus elastica decora Roxb. ex Hornem. 'Decora'		Moraceae	c. (Himalaya, Indonesia)
Ficus rubiginosa Desf. ex Vent.		Moraceae	Oceania
Ficus x 'Schrijveriana'		Moraceae	Hybrid
Gasteria stayneri Poelln.		Liliaceae	South Africa
Haemanthus albiflos Jacq.		Amaryllidaceae	South Africa
Hedera helix L. 'Oro di Bogliasco'		Araliaceae	cv. (Europe, Russia)
Hibiscus rosa sinensis L.	Hibiscus	Malvaceae	Tropical Asia
Howea forsteriana (C. Moore & F. Muell.) Becc.	Kentia	Palmae	Lord Howe Islands
Hoya carnosa (L.f.) R. Br.	Wax flower	Asclepiadaceae	Europe
Hoya carnosa (L.f.) R.Br. 'Variegata'		Asclepiadaceae	cv. (Europe)
Hypoestes phyllostachya Bak.		Acanthaceae	South Africa, Madagascar, Asia
Jacobinia carnea (Lindl.) Nichols.		Acanthaceae	Brasil
Jasminum officinale L.		Oleaceae	Asia Minor, Himalaya, China
Kalanchoe beharensis Drake		Crassulaceae	Madagascar

Kalanchoe blossfeldiana Poelln.		Crassulaceae	Madagascar
Kalanchoe longiflora Schldl.		Crassulaceae	South Africa
Kalanchoe tomentosa Bak.		Crassulaceae	Madagascar
Kalanchoe tubiflora (Harv.) Hamet		Crassulaceae	Madagascar, South Africa
Kleinia articulata (L. f.) Haw.		Compositae	South Africa
Kleinia stapeliiformis (E. Phillips) Stapf.		Compositae	Somalia
Lantana camara L.		Verbenaceae	Tropical America
Leuchtenbergia principis Hook.		Cactaceae	Mexico
Mammillaria angularis Link & Otto ex Pfeiff.		Cactaceae	Mexico
Mammillaria hahniana Werderm.		Cactaceae	Mexico
Maranta leuconeura E. Morr. var. *kerchoviana*		Marantaceae	Brasil
Passiflora edulis Sims		Passifloraceae	Brasil
Mimosa pudica L.	Mimosa	Leguminosae	Central America, Oceania
Medinilla magnifica Lindl.		Melastomataceae	Filippines
Monstera deliciosa Liebm.		Araceae	Central America
Muehlenbeckia platyclada (F. Muell.) Meissn.		Polygonaceae	Salomon Islands
Musa basjoo Sieb. & Zucc.	Japanese banana	Musaceae	Japan
Neoregelia carolinae (Beer.) L.B. Sm. 'Meyendorffii'		Bromeliaceae	cv.(Brasil)
Nephrolepis exaltata (L.) Schott. 'Muscosa'		Oleandraceae	cv. (Pantropical)
Nephrolepis exaltata (L.) Schott. 'Rooseveltii Plumosa'		Oleandraceae	cv. (Pantropical)
Nephrolepis exaltata (L.) Schott. 'Smithii'		Oleandraceae	cv. (Pantropical)
Nephrolepis exaltata (L.) Schott. 'Teddyi Junior'		Oleandraceae	cv. (Pantropical)
Nolina recurvata (Lem.) Hemsl.	Smoke-eating plant	Liliaceae	Mexico
Nopalea cochenillifera (L.) Salm-Dyck		Cactaceae	Mexico
Oncidium incurvum Barker ex Lindl.		Orchidaceae	Mexico
Opuntia cylindrica (Lam.) DC.		Cactaceae	Mexico
Opuntia leucotricha DC.		Cactaceae	Ecuador
Opuntia microdasys (Lehm.) Pfeiff.		Cactaceae	Mexico
Opuntia vulgaris (Willd.) Haw. 'Variegata'		Cactaceae	Mexico
Opuntia monacantha (Willd.) Haw.		Cactaceae	cv. (Brasil, Argentina)
Oreopanax capitatus Decne & Planch.	Batavian aralia	Araliaceae	Brasil, Argentina
Pachyphytum brevifolium Rose.		Crassulaceae	South America
Pachyphytum oviferum Purpus.		Crassulaceae	Mexico
Pelargonium peltatum (L.) L'Hérit.		Geraniaceae	Mexico
Pelargonium radula L'Hérit.		Geraniaceae	South Africa
Pelargonium tomentosum Jacq.		Geraniaceae	South Africa
Peperomia arifolia Miq.		Piperaceae	South Africa
Peperomia magnoliifolia (Jacq.) Dietr.		Piperaceae	Brasil, Paraguay, Argentina
Peperomia magnoliifolia (Jacq.) Dietr. 'Green & Gold'		Piperaceae	South America, East Indies)
Peperomia trinervula C. DC.		Piperaceae	cv. (South America, East Indies)
Persea americana Mill.	Avocado	Lauraceae	South America
Philodendron mamei André		Araceae	Central America
Philodendron scandens K. Koch & Sello.		Araceae	Ecuador
Philodendron Schott. x 'Red Emerald'		Araceae	South America
Philodendron Schott. x 'Emerald Queen'		Araceae	Hybrid
Philodendron selloum K. Koch		Araceae	Hybrid
Pilea cadierei Gagnep. & Guillaum. 'Compacta'		Urticaceae	Brasil
Platycerium biforcatum (Cav.) C. Chr.		Polypodiaceae	Vietnam
Platycerium grande (Fée) Kunze		Polypodiaceae	Asia, Polynesia, Australia
Pleiospilos simulans (Marloth) N.E. Br.		Aizoaceae	Malaysia, Australia, Filippines
Polypodium aureum L. 'Subauriculatum'		Polypodiaceae	South Africa
Portulacaria afra Jacq.		Portulacaceae	Tropical America
Raphidophora decursiva (Wallich.) Schott.		Araceae	South Africa
Rhipsalis cereoides (Backeb. & Voll.) Cast.		Cactaceae	Central Asia, Sri Lanka
Rhipsalis mesembryanthemoides Haw.		Cactaceae	Brasil
Russelia equisetiformis Schldl. & Cham.		Scrophulariaceae	Brasil
Sansevieria trifasciata hort. ex. Prain. 'Hahnii'		Agavaceae	Mexico
Sansevieria trifasciata hort. ex. Prain. 'Laurentii'		Liliaceae	cv. (Nigeria)
Sedum morganianum Walth.		Crassulaceae	cv. (Nigeria)
Sedum weinbergii (Rose) A. Berger		Crassulaceae	Mexico
Sobralia macrantha Lindl.		Orchidaceae	Mexico
Solanum pseudocapsicum L.		Solanaceae	Central America
Tibouchina urvilleana (DC) Cogn.		Melastomataceae	Madeira
Stanhopea wardii Lodd. ex Lindl.		Orchidaceae	Brasil
Strelitzia alba (l.) Skeels.		Musaceae	Central America
Strelitzia reginae Banks ex Dryand.		Musaceae	South Africa
Strobilanthes dyerianus Mast.		Acanthaceae	South Africa
Tetrapanax papyrifer (Hook.) K. Koch.	Rice paper	Araliaceae	Burma
Tradescantia fluminensis Vell. Conc. 'Variegata'		Commelinaceae	Taiwan
Tradescantia navicularis Ortgies.		Commelinaceae	Brasil
Tradescantia pallida (Rose) D. Hunt.		Commelinaceae	Mexico
Tradescantia zebrina hort. ex Bosse.		Commelinaceae	Mexico
Vanda tricolor Lindl.		Orchidaceae	Mexico
Vriesea splendens (Brongn.) Lem.		Bromeliaceae	Java, Laos
Xanthosoma sagittifolium (L.) Schott.		Araceae	South America
Xanthosoma violaceum Schott.		Araceae	Tropics
Zygocactus truncatus (Haw.) Schum.		Cactaceae	Tropics

Paolo Cottini wishes to thank Massimiliano Pozzi and Eliseo Bianchi for their cooperation
Paola Zatti wishes to thank Fernando Mazzocca who kindly provided us with his published material on the subject

Photo Credits
The photographs that illustrate this guide were taken by Paolo Cottini for the Garden,
and by Vittorio Calore for the Villa and the Museum, with the exception of photographs from the
Pizzi Archives pp. 4, 5, 9, 10, 56, 57

Project management and publication of the guide by
Arti Grafiche Amilcare Pizzi S.p.A.

Editor in-chief: Dario Cimorelli
Project co-cordinators: Roberta Concas, Francesco Mandressi
Translation from the Italian: Sylvia Notini
Pagination: Massimo Strada
Cover design: Studio Camuffo, Venezia
© 2000 by Silvana Editoriale

Distribution
Silvana Editoriale S.p.A.

Via Margherita De Vizzi, 86
20092 Cinisello Balsamo (MI)
Tel. 02 6172464-02 66046005
Fax 02 6172464
www.silvanaeditoriale.it

Reproductions, printing, and binding are
the work of Arti Grafiche Amilcare Pizzi S.p.A.
Cinisello Balsamo (Milan)

Printed in June 2000